# INDUSTRIAL PSYCHOLOGY
# RESEARCH TRENDS

# INDUSTRIAL PSYCHOLOGY RESEARCH TRENDS

INA M. PEARLE
EDITOR

Nova Science Publishers, Inc.
*New York*

**LIBRARY OF CONGRESS CATALOGING-IN-PUBLICATION DATA**

Industrial psychology research trends / Ina M. Pearle (editor).
   p. cm.
Includes index.
ISBN-13: 978-1-60021-825-5 (hardcover)
ISBN-10: 1-60021-825-3 (hardcover)
1. Psychology, Industrial.  I. Pearle, Ina M.
HF5548.8.I5237                  2006
158.7--dc22             2007024499

*Published by Nova Science Publishers, Inc. ✤New York*

# CONTENTS

# PREFACE

Industrial and organizational psychology (also known as I/O psychology, work psychology, work and organizational psychology, W-O psychology, occupational psychology, or personnel psychology) concerns the application of psychological theories, research methods, and intervention strategies to workplace issues. I/O psychologists are interested in making organizations more productive while ensuring workers are able to lead physically and psychologically healthy lives. Relevant topics include personnel psychology, motivation and leadership, employee selection, training, and development, organization development and guided change, organizational behavior, and work and family issues. This new book presents leading research from around the globe in this field.

Chapter 1 - The purpose of this study was to examine the extent to which self-efficacy for adapting to organizational transitions would buffer the negative effects of job insecurity. According to Bandura (1982), positive affective and behavioral outcomes can be expected only when self-efficacy and outcome expectancies are judged to be positive. Thus, it was predicted that self-efficacy would serve to buffer the stress of working in an organization undergoing a major transition, but only when the employee's outcome expectancy (i.e., perception of job security) was positive. Results indicate high self-efficacy was related to more positive attitudinal and behavioral outcomes (i.e., affective reactions, organizational commitment, self-reported physical health, and withdrawal intentions). However, the positive effects of self-efficacy were attenuated when outcome expectancies were low (i.e., when employees perceived their jobs to be insecure). These results suggest organizations should increase communication during times of organizational transition to improve the accuracy of job security perceptions and to increase the extent to which employees feel capable of handling pending organizational changes.

Chapter 2 - Despite the increased use of mid-level health care providers in an effort to save money and fill gaps in physician shortages there has been little examination of their experience of medical resistance. Examining this is important because the extent of collaboration can influence job satisfaction, retention, inter-professional relations and patient care. This study explored the extent to which mid-level providers experienced medical resistance though qualitative semi-structured interviews with 59 health care providers (nurse practitioners (NPs), nurse anesthetists (CRNAs), physician assistants (PAs) and key informants). The results suggest that the amount of resistance varied by gender, type of provider and the extent of 'substitutability.' Jurisdictional disputes seemed most evident around the areas that were most valued by physicians, while there was less resistance around the fringes. Key tensions arose around financial concerns and maintaining medical dominance, while some physicians resisted because they lacked knowledge of the role. Mid-level providers experienced resistance from both the political level and in day-to-day practice. Each of the providers varied in the extent to which they considered themselves a substitute provider. CRNAs saw themselves as substitute providers more often than a complement, while NPs were somewhat mixed. Meanwhile, PAs viewed themselves as a complement provider more often than a substitute. Those who considered themselves a 'complementary' provider reported less resistance compared to those who considered themselves a substitute. There were three key areas where physicians did not put up as much resistance towards mid-level providers: devalued tasks, less desirable patient groups and devalued geographical locations. In conclusion, the extent of resistance experienced by mid-level providers varied by the extent of 'substitutability' of the provider and also by gender.

Chapter 3 - This chapter reviews extant literature on mental health in the workplace. The authors give particular attention to different models of work stress and explain its relationship with job burnout and depression which are two common mental health problems at work. Although the tie between stress and mental health is well known, there is a dearth of research on exploring its relationship in specific occupations. In the second part of this book chapter, the authors present a case study on identifying the work stress of professionals working in the financial services section in Hong Kong. Finally, suggestions are made as to research that needs to be conducted in the future with a view to raising the awareness of employers and employees on this issue and at the same time unveiling the possible etiologies, promoting good mental health practices, and maintaining a healthy working environment.

Chapter 4 - The driving behavior of most drivers is sub-optimal concerning fuel consumption. However, little is known of how important different sources of waste are in terms of how common such behavior is on the road. This question was studied in a small sample of logging truck drivers for the variables idling, high speed, shifting gear, rpm and braking, with various statistical methods. In multiple regressions it was found that the studied factors explained a large part of the existing variance. Also, the ranking of the studied factors as to their relative importance as sources of waste differed depending on the method of analysis used, indicating that exactly how the question is put to the same data can shape the answer. The results have implications for training of drivers in fuel-efficient driving, as well as for the development of support tools and driving cycles.

Chapter 5 - It is well known that job stress influences employees' work satisfaction, physical and mental health and well-being. The present paper includes results of two independent studies. First, the authors have analyzed the potential influencing characteristics of work environment related to nurses' life satisfaction with special emphasis put on burnout factors. Second, the next study has been to look at the relationship between psychosocial work environment and self-perceived health in a sample of health care staff living and working in Subotica, Serbia. In the first study, there were 201 registered nurses working in Szeged hospitals, Hungary. In the second study, there were 253 health care workers in the sample, most of them worked as registered nurses, head nurses or assistants (altogether 80.1% of them). The data collection was going on by means of self-administered questionnaires. The health care staff as respondents report a high frequency of experiencing emotionally provoking situations. Parallel with this, they often lack the social network which would provide effective support in these situations. The frequencies of emotionally provoking situations and the lack of social support, together with the paid extra work and the low levels of work satisfaction influence negatively their self-perceived health. Findings also suggest that burnout factors are significantly related to life satisfaction, the relationship is particularly strong with emotional exhaustion. Work satisfaction shows a strong relationship with the three burnout subscales, in addition, the relationship between life satisfaction and work satisfaction is particularly strong. These results draw the attention to the role of psychosocial work environment in determining satisfaction with life as an indicator of subjective well-being. In addition, the psychosocial work environment significantly has an impact on the health care workers' self-perceived health and their levels of psychosomatic symptoms. There is a great need of learning skills and techniques among health care staff which would help them in preventing deterioration of their psychological health and well-being.

Chapter 6 - Night and shiftwork affect the workers' health and psychosocial well-being, due to the disruption of biological rhythms and difficulties adjusting to sociofamily life. Problems related to those work schedules are unavoidable, since working at odd hours is not compatible with the diurnal pattern of the human body and the organization of society. The financial "basic compensation" adopted worldwide is obviously not enough to compensate workers for the inconveniences related to night and shiftwork, as an extra payment does not help them to deal with health hazards, sleep deprivation or to family disruption associated with working non-diurnal shifts. This is why there is a general agreement among researchers that intervention measures should focus on the effective reduction of the impact of these work schedules. There is no general way to achieve this goal. Actually, the selection of measures depends on the specific situation, with emphasis on the reduction of human and social costs by means of measures towards each type of hazard. Thus, intervention measures are not definitive solutions to problems, but instead can be viewed as recommendations and strategies implemented by employees and employers to reduce difficulties related to workers' health and well-being. Such recommendations deal with aspects related to work organization, so as to reduce the demands for shiftwork (mainly night work and irregular working times), or to implement work schemes that imply less problems to workers. Intervention measures also refer to changes in the work environment as, for instance, providing round-the-clock canteens with adequate meals for night workers. Measures aiming at the adjustment of biological rhythms to the work schedule are based on chronobiological principles, such as those related to melatonin ingestion or exposure to bright light. Whatever the action to be adopted, the educational perspective and the participative approach seem to be relevant in dealing with challenges related to night and shiftwork, as judged by successful interventions in several industries and service sectors.

In: Industrial Psychology Research Trends
Editor: Ina M. Pearle, pp. 1-4

ISBN: 978-1-60021-825-5
© 2007 Nova Science Publishers, Inc.

*Expert Commentary A*

# THE IMPACT OF 'EXPERT PATIENT' AND SELF-CARE INITIATIVES ON HEALTH CARE PERSONNEL

## Sally Lindsay[*]

Institute for Social, Cultural and Policy Research;
University of Salford, Salford United Kingdom; M5 4QA

Health and illness experts have sharpened the realisation of the extent to which the management of chronic conditions is not in the direct control of health professionals but rather in that of patients and their informal carers. Chronic conditions are the cause of poor health and disability and are now one of the leading causes of death. This is concerning to health policy leaders because as many one in three people may be living with a chronic disease (Department of Health 2005). Chronic illness places a huge economic burden on patients and informal carers, the health care system and the labour market. Current health policy encourages patients to become 'experts' in the self-management of their conditions in the belief that it will help save costs and improve health and well-being. The notion of the 'expert patient', referring to those who manage their own illnesses and conditions by developing knowledge relevant to maintaining health and minimizing illness is pivotal to government plans to modernise the health care systems by linking patient expertise to ideas of empowerment, a better quality of life and a user-driven health care system (Fox et al. 2005).

Although expert patient initiatives have many implications for patients, there has been much less attention given to the impact this has for health care personnel, especially from an industrial psychology perspective. Most of the research in this area focuses on physicians' and nurses' ability to influence patients and to empower them to become more active in their self-care and not the impact this may have on health care providers themselves. Examining the implications of expert patient initiatives is salient because health care personnel comprise a high proportion of the labour force. There are several key areas that need further exploration

---

[*] Sally Lindsay: Email: s.lindsay@salford.ac.uk

which include the impact of expert patients on: (1) health care providers' continuing education; (2) professional autonomy; (3) workload and job satisfaction; and (4) inter-professional relations.

From a health care provider's perspective, encouraging self-care is more than simply providing information to patients. It is also about educating patients about how to take care of their illness (Department of Health 2005). Indeed, patients often want more information from their health providers about how to manage their illness. Professionals guiding self-management need to continually update and maintain the skills necessary to encourage self-care (Lambert et al. 2000). Thus, the rise in expert patients and the self-management of chronic illness has implications for training health care providers (Blakeman et al. 2006; McDonald and Gibson 2006). This is important for all types of health care providers as they must remain up-to-date on trends and are increasingly expected to react to web print-outs that their patients show them.

Expert patients also present a challenge to health care providers' autonomy. Previous research has shown that clinicians need to be trained to increase their support of patient autonomy (Williams et al. 2005), yet little is known about what health care providers' reaction is to this. Until recently, the medical profession has maintained its autonomy and dominance over the health care division of labour. The rise of expert patient initiatives, however, presents a challenge to medical dominance and professional authority.

In a qualitative study by Blakeman et al. (2006), GPs reported both tensions and trade-offs in respect to their role in facilitating self-management. They found that although GPs valued patient involvement they felt it was in conflict with their professional responsibility. Contextual factors also limited the extent to which physicians could encourage self-management (Blakeman et al. 2006).

Nurses also play a major role in assisting patients with chronic diseases to manage their symptoms, adhere to treatment and change behaviour (Kodiath and Shively 2005; Redman 2005). Wilson et al (2006) found that nurses were most anxious about expert patients compared to other health professionals, which may have been due to a lack of confidence and a fear of litigation. Their study found that apart from nurse specialists most nurses were limited in appropriately facilitating self-management, which may be a result of the nursing culture tending to see patients as passive along with an over-emphasis on empirical knowledge (Wilson et al. 2006). Future research should examine how expert patients are influencing autonomy and power relations not only with physicians but other health care providers as well. Further examination is also needed into how expert patients are influencing health care providers' workloads, job satisfaction and stress levels.

Another key area that expert patients have influenced is patient-provider relations. Successful self-care is based on having access to quality information, good knowledge-processing skills and the right social networks. Evidence shows that shared decision-making can help improve outcomes (Gravel et al 206) but what do health care providers think about involving patients in treatment decisions and relinquishing some of their control? Although some research suggests that shared decision making leads to improved patient-provider communication (McMath 2004; Terry and Healey 2000) more examination is needed of the impact that this is having on all types of health care providers and not just physicians.

Effective disease management requires patients and health care professionals to collaborate in the development of self-management plans (Anderson and Funnell 2005). Supporting expert patients requires an increase in inter-professional collaboration (Amost and

Laschinger 2002), yet there has been relatively little examination of how expert patients are influencing inter-professional relations. The main providers of chronic disease care are primary care teams (GPs, practice nurses and health care assistants), community nurses, pharmacists, dieticians, opticians, podiatrists and physiotherapists (Department of Health 2005), yet most research in this area focuses on physicians while less is known about other types of health care providers. Specific attention needs to be paid to role boundaries, inter-professional conflict, collaboration and workload. Although some of the above issues have been explored from a health care perspective, very little work has been done from an industrial psychology perspective. Psychology can help shed light on the impact of the expert patient agenda by opening the debate in several key areas affecting health care personnel.

## REFERENCES

Amost, J. and Laschinger, H. (2002) Workplace empowerment, collaborative work relationships, and job strain in nurse practitioners. *Journal of the American Academy of Nurse Practitioners.* 14 (9): 408-419.

Anderson, R and Funnell, M. (2005) Patient empowerment: reflections on the challenge of fostering the adoption of a new paradigm. *Patient Education and Counseling.* 57(2): 153-157.

Blakeman, T., Macdonald, W., Bower, P., Gately, C., and Chew-Graham, C. (2006) A qualitative study of GPs' attitudes to self-management of chronic disease. *British Journal of General Practice.* 56(527): 407-414.

Department of Health. (2005) *Supporting People with Long Term Conditions.* Leeds: Primary Care DOH.

Fox N, K Ward and A O'Rourke. (2005) The 'expert patient.' *Social Science and Medicine.* 60: 1299-1309.

Gravel, F., Legare F, and Graham I. (2006) Barriers and facilitators to implementing shared decision-making in clinical practice: a systematic review of health professionals' perceptions. *Implementation Science.* 1: 16.

Kodiath, M, Kelly, A, and Shively M. (2005) Improving quality of life in patients with chronic heart failure. *Journal of Cardiovascular Nursing.* 20(1): 43-48.

Lambert, B., Butin, D., Moran, D. Zhao, S., Carr, B. Chen, C. and Kizis, F. 2000. Arthritis care: comparison of physicians' and patients' views. *Seminars in Arthritis and Rheumatisim.* 30(2): 100-10.

McDonald, V. and Gibson, P. (2006) Asthma self-management and education. *Chronic Respiratory Disease.* 3(1): 29-37.

McMath, E. and Harvey, C. (2004) Complex wounds: a partnership approach to patient documentation. *British Journal of Nursing.* 13(11): S12-6.

Redman, B. (2005) The ethics of self-management preparation for chronic illness. *Nursing Ethics.* 12(4): 360-369.

Terry, P. and Healey, M. (2000) The physician's role in educating patients. *Journal of Family Practice.* 49(4): 314-318.

Williams, G., McGregor, H., King, D., Nelson, C., Glasgow, R. (2005) Variation in perceived competence, glycemic control and patient satisfaction: relationship to autonomy support from physicians. *Patient Education and Counseling.* 57(1): 39-45.

Wilson, P., Kendall, S., Brooks, F. (2006) Nurses' responses to expert patients. *International Journal of Nursing Studies.* 43: 803-818.

In: Industrial Psychology Research Trends
Editor: Ina M. Pearle, pp. 5-8

ISBN: 978-1-60021-825-5
© 2007 Nova Science Publishers, Inc.

*Expert Commentary B*

# FUEL-EFFICIENT DRIVING RESEARCH: AN AREA IN NEED OF EXPLORATION

*A. E. af Wåhlberg*

Dept. of Psychology, Uppsala University; Sweden

## INTRODUCTION

In our energy-hungry world, large quantities of this much-wanted commodity is simply wasted. This is perhaps nowhere as apparent as in transportation; the endless congestions, where idling engines consume tons of petrol and spew pollutants, are there for everyone to see in industrialized countries all over the world. Still, very little is being made about the main problem; human behavior. Politicians and bureaucrats are mainly discussing technical solutions, involving ever more sophisticated ways of converting energy into forms that we can use. Meanwhile, our capability of handling this energy is still at a very primitive level. If we have it, we spend it.

In this commentary, it will be argued that at least 50 percent of the fuel used by private car drivers is spent unnecessarily, and that this waste will not be diminished by the technical solutions of today, but that radically new ways of designing energy-using equipment must be found. In general, the main goal should be to alter human behavior at the core; our hitherto unstoppable urge is to use every resource we have until it hurts. This is also where research comes into the picture. We simply need to know more about how and why humans waste what they have, and how these behaviors can be altered.

## DRIVING: AN EXAMPLE OF FUEL WASTING BEHAVIORS

Although there is precious little research on people's driving behavior in terms of fuel consumption, all of it would seem to point in the same direction; almost all drivers waste fuel unnecessarily. Two categories can be distinguished; behaviors at the strategic (mainly trip planning), and tactical level (actual driving). Each of these can be further subdivided and analyzed, and need different tactics when it is to be battled.

At the most basic level of (individual) strategic travel planning, it can be asked; do we really need to go anywhere? Next, what modes of travel are available? What routes? The available research would seem to indicate that, very often, travel is undertaken unnecessarily. For example, Hake and Foxx (1978) achieved ten and twenty percent reductions of travel in two test groups by the use of reinforcement and record keeping.

At the level of actual driving, the saving potential is in the range of tens of percent, as shown by training sessions (af Wåhlberg, 2002), experiments (Laurell, 1985) and on-road behavior (Nader, 1991). Fuel is burned for idling, braking and high speeds (af Wåhlberg and Göthe, this volume), variables that are to a large degree under the volitional control of the driver. These wasteful behaviors can also be changed (Runnion, Watson and McWorther, 1978; Siero, Boon, Kok and Siero, 1989), although less than half of the potential would seem to be the result (af Wåhlberg, 2006; in press).

Finally, at both levels of driving, Rothstein (1980) achieved a thirty percent reduction of fuel consumption by television feedback. As fuel data were taken from gas stations, it is not possible to know how drivers achieved this, but it was a result of a televised campaign with tips on fuel conservation. Again, what was shown was the potential for saving, or the large degree of unnecessary use.

## THE REBOUND EFFECT

The catch with all the technical (and some of the behavioral) solutions to fuel waste is that we probably get an opposing effect when consumption per mile is decreased. Most people will probably react by traveling more. However, this is a long-term effect that is hard to discern if one does not specifically go looking for it. So far, few researchers seem to have been interested in this type of question.

Economists have been doing research on what they call the 'rebound' effect on fuel consumption (e.g. Small and van Dender, 2007; Herring and Roy, in press), which is the increase in fuel use when more efficient means of using it are introduced. However, the rebound effect seems to have been the exclusive habitat of economists and similar researchers, using methods that may not be very well suited for the problem studied. First, the mathematics tend to be somewhat advanced, including a great many assumptions, none of which seem to be empirically founded (e.g. Brännlund, Ghalwash and Nordström, 2007; Small and van Dender, 2007). Second, the data used typically seem to be at a very aggregated (often nation-) level, making them vulnerable to all sorts of effects that are not empirically controlled for. Also, researchers in this area do not seem to test whether their estimates of gasoline prices or engine efficiency are valid.

It can here be noted that not only is the economical perspective not sufficient when it comes to studying the problem of energy waste, but that it also has few methods available, with little power to change human behavior. Prices and legislation are simply not that powerful, because people will tend to find ways of circumventing laws, and costs are not that strong a determinant of fuel consumption anyway.

## MAKING ENERGY CONSUMPTION VISIBLE

One of the main problems of energy waste is probably that humans are not very adept at associating between their own actions and fuel consumption. They simply cannot see that their own behavior is wasteful. This is probably due to two factors; feedback is late, and it is in many instances in an aggregated and absolute form.

Humans have a hard time understanding delayed feedback. We are simply geared to make inferences about causality over very short time frames. Actually, the timing is often all there is to it, and we can start believing in cause and effect just because two phenomena happened very close in time to each other. Concerning energy, we cannot perceive how much more energy we use when we turn up the heat or drive very erratically, because this only show up at the heating bill and the gas station. The vehicle computers showing fuel consumption, which are becoming standard, are a big step forward here. However, they do not today solve the problem of the absolute value of the information.

It can be suspected that people are seldom aware of how their energy consumption is related to what is actually achievable, or how their wastefulness compare to others. Given that they just get an electricity or fuel bill, the only values they can relate to are their own of previous months. This tells them very little about what is possible, and there is thus little incentive for them to act differently.

## ESTABLISHING A NEW FIELD OF RESEARCH; ENERGY PSYCHOLOGY

It is here suggested that to battle the energy wasting tendencies of humans, we need knowledge about how and why this happens. Therefore, research must be undertaken which focuses on how and why people use their resources, and the change of their behaviors. This should be done on the individual level, because the aggregated data used by economists are probably not very well suited for this question, and the behavior change methods used by psychologists for decades can be applied at this level. Thus, a new field should be established; energy and resource psychology, because it is the individual who waste our resources, and it is within psychology that the necessary knowledge can be found.

## REFERENCES

Brännlund, R., Ghalwash, T., and Nordström, J. (2007). Increased energy efficiency and the rebound effect: Effects on consumption and emissions. *Energy Economics*, 29, 1-17.

Hake, D. F., and Foxx, R. M. (1978). Promoting gasoline conservation: The effects of reinforcement schedules, a leader and self-recording. *Behavior Modification*, 2, 339-369.

Herring, H., and Roy, R. (in press). Technological innovation, energy efficient design and the rebound effect. *Technovation*.

Laurell, H. (1985). *Körsättets betydelse för bränsleförbrukningen.* VTI-rapport 298.

Linköping. [*The influence of driving style on fuel consumption.* VTI-report 298]. Swedish National Road

Nader, J. (1991). Measurement of the impact of driving technique on fuel consumption: Preliminary results. *Roads and Transportation,* Technical Note. TN-172, 1-6.

Rothstein, R. N. (1980). Television feedback used to modify gasoline consumption. *Behavior Therapy*, 11, 683-688

Runnion, A., Watson, J. D., and McWorther, J. (1978). Energy savings in interstate transportation through feedback. *Journal of Organizational Behaviour Management*, 1, 180-191.

Siero, S., Boon, M., Kok, G., and Siero, F. (1989). Modification of driving behaviour in a large transport organization: A field experiment. *Journal of Applied Psychology*, 74, 417-423.

Small, K. A., and van Dender, K. (2007). Fuel efficiency and motor vehicle travel: The declining rebound effect. *The Energy Journal*, 28, 25-51.

af Wåhlberg, A. E. (2006). Short-term effects of training in economical driving; passenger comfort and driver acceleration behavior. *International Journal of Industrial Ergonomics*, 36, 151-163.

af Wåhlberg, A. E. (in press). Long term effects of training in economical driving; fuel consumption, accidents, driver acceleration behavior and technical feedback. *International Journal of Industrial Ergonomics,*

af Wåhlberg, A. E., and Göthe, J. (this volume). *Fuel wasting behaviors of truck drivers*. Nova.

In: Industrial Psychology Research Trends
Editor: Ina M. Pearle, pp. 9-21
ISBN: 978-1-60021-825-5
© 2007 Nova Science Publishers, Inc.

*Chapter 1*

# SELF-EFFICACY FOR ADAPTING TO ORGANIZATIONAL TRANSITIONS: IT HELPS, BUT ONLY WHEN THE PROSPECTS ARE BRIGHT

## *Tahira M. Probst*[*]

Washington State University, Vancouver, Canada

## ABSTRACT

The purpose of this study was to examine the extent to which self-efficacy for adapting to organizational transitions would buffer the negative effects of job insecurity. According to Bandura (1982), positive affective and behavioral outcomes can be expected only when self-efficacy and outcome expectancies are judged to be positive. Thus, it was predicted that self-efficacy would serve to buffer the stress of working in an organization undergoing a major transition, but only when the employee's outcome expectancy (i.e., perception of job security) was positive. Results indicate high self-efficacy was related to more positive attitudinal and behavioral outcomes (i.e., affective reactions, organizational commitment, self-reported physical health, and withdrawal intentions). However, the positive effects of self-efficacy were attenuated when outcome expectancies were low (i.e., when employees perceived their jobs to be insecure). These results suggest organizations should increase communication during times of organizational transition to improve the accuracy of job security perceptions and to increase the extent to which employees feel capable of handling pending organizational changes.

[*] Address correspondence to: Tahira M. Probst; Assistant Professor, Department of Psychology; Washington State University at Vancouver; 14204 NE Salmon Creek Avenue; Vancouver, WA 98686; Tel. (360) 546-9746; E-mail: probst@vancouver.wsu.edu; Web: http://www.vancouver.wsu.edu/fac/probst

# SELF-EFFICACY FOR ADAPTING TO ORGANIZATIONAL TRANSITIONS: IT HELPS, BUT ONLY WHEN THE PROSPECTS ARE BRIGHT

Economic rumblings throughout the globe, accompanied by ever-increasing levels of domestic and international competition, government deregulation of industry, and the fast pace of organizational technology change have placed extreme financial pressure on virtually every sector of the American economy. In response, organizations have engaged in several strategies to tighten their corporate belts and remain competitive: organizational restructuring, formation of mergers with or acquisition of rival competitors, and voluntary or involuntary workforce reductions. Annually, approximately 500,000 U.S. employees can expect to lose their jobs as a result of these transitions (Simons, 1998). Thus, these numbers are not the product of an anomalous year, but rather reflect a new organizational trend of reducing corporate expenses through such organizational transitions.

Organizational transitions can lead to numerous job stressors. Role conflict can increase. Role ambiguity can ensue. But, perhaps the most prevalent stressor during time of major organizational transition is that of job insecurity (Ashford, Lee, and Bobko, 1989; Buessing, 1986; Davy, Kinicki, and Scheck. 1991; Greenhalgh and Rosenblatt, 1984). A growing body of literature suggests that job insecurity results in many negative consequences for employees who perceive their jobs to be at risk. Employees suffer from decreased job satisfaction (Ashford, Lee, and Bobko, 1989; Davy, Kinicki, and Scheck, 1991; Probst, 1998), a greater incidence of reported health conditions (Brenner et al., 1983; Cottington, et al., 1986; Dooley, Rook, and Catalano, 1987; Kuhnert, Sims, and Lahey, 1989; Probst, 1998; Roskies and Louis-Guerin, 1990), and decreased mental health (Dekker and Schaufeli, 1995; Probst, 1998). Not surprisingly, organizations do not emerge unscathed either. The more dissatisfied employees are with their perceived job security, the more negative affective reactions they have to workplace transitions (Probst, 1998), the more likely they are to quit their job (Ashford, Lee, and Bobko, 1989; Davy, Kinicki, and Scheck, 1991; Probst, 1998), the less committed they are to the organization (Ashford, Lee, and Bobko, 1989; Davy, Kinicki, and Scheck, 1991; Probst, 1998), and the more frequently they engage in work withdrawal behaviors such as absenteeism, tardiness, and work task avoidance (Probst, 1998). Finally, recent research also suggests that as workers become more fearful for their jobs, less emphasis is placed on safety, and worker injuries and accidents can increase (Probst and Brubaker, 2001).

The purpose of this study was to examine the extent to which self-efficacy for adapting to organizational transitions would buffer some of these negative effects of job insecurity. Based on the theory of self-efficacy, it was predicted that self-efficacy would serve to buffer the stress of working in an organization undergoing a major transition, but only when the employee's outcome expectancy was positive.

## The Theory of Self-Efficacy

According to the theory of self-efficacy (Bandura, 1982), perceived self-efficacy is the extent to which an individual judges him- or herself capable of dealing with a prospective situation. Perceived self-efficacy can explain individual differences in the reaction to stress.

Those who have a strong sense of self-efficacy exert greater effort to meet challenges, whereas those with low self-efficacy tend to magnify personal deficiencies and the severity of potential threats (Beck, 1976; Lazarus and Launier, 1978). As a result, self-referent reservations create a high level of cognitively generated stress (Bandura, 1982). On the other hand, those with a strong sense of self-efficacy deploy greater effort in the face of adversity.

While knowledge of an individual's self-efficacy is central to understanding that individual's response to a stressful situation, knowing the individual's assessment of potential situational outcomes is essential as well. Outcome expectancy is the belief that certain behaviors will lead to particular outcomes (Sherer, Maddux, Mercandante, Prentice-Dunn, Jacobs, and Rogers, 1982). According to Bandura (1982), both self-efficacy and outcome expectancies exert a powerful influence on behavior and affective reactions. People may have a feeling of futility because they doubt they have the capacity to do what is required. They may also give up trying, not because they believe themselves to be incapable, but because they expect their efforts will not produce the desired results due to the unresponsiveness of the environment.

According to Bandura (1982), positive affective and behavioral outcomes can be expected only when self-efficacy and outcome expectancies are judged to be positive. When either self-efficacy expectancies or outcome expectancies are low, resignation, apathy, despondency, or withdrawal can ensue. Thus, in the current study, it was expected that employees must be confident regarding both outcome expectancies in the form of perceived job security and self-efficacy beliefs with respect to one's ability to adapt to the pending organizational transition for positive affective and behavioral outcomes to result.

## Self-Efficacy for Adapting to Organizational Transitions

Self-efficacy for adapting to organizational transitions was defined as the extent to which an employee judged him- or herself capable of possessing the ability to meet the challenges associated with major organizational changes. Individuals who judge themselves incapable of adapting to organizational transitions (e.g., organizational mergers or acquisitions, new policies, coworkers, and/or supervisors, changes in individual responsibilities) are predicted to inflate the severity of threat that such organizational changes hold for them, and consequently experience higher job dissatisfaction, more negative affective reactions, and a higher incidence of negative consequences. On the other hand, individuals who anticipate they possess the requisite knowledge, skills, and abilities needed to cope with organizational change are expected to exert greater effort to meet the challenges they face (Bandura and Schunk, 1981), and consequently experience (1) more positive affective outcomes in the form of higher job satisfaction, more organizational commitment, and fewer negative affective reactions to the organizational transition and (2) more positive behavioral outcomes in the form of fewer turnover intentions and less work withdrawal.

## Hypotheses

Based on the literature reviewed above, three hypotheses were generated. The first hypothesis predicted a main effect of self-efficacy, such that:

Hypothesis 1: High self-efficacy individuals are predicted to have more positive job attitudes and fewer negative affective reactions to work events than low self-efficacy individuals.

In addition, given the substantial body of literature on the negative consequences of job insecurity reviewed above, it was expected that the more an individual perceives their job to be insecure, the more negative the employee's affective and behavioral outcomes. Thus,

Hypothesis 2: Low perceived job security is predicted to be related to more negative affective and behavioral outcomes.

Finally, given the theoretical expectation regarding the interactive nature of self-efficacy judgments and outcome expectancy judgments, it was also predicted that:

Hypothesis 3: The positive effects of self-efficacy will be greater under conditions of high perceived job security.

In order to test these predictions, employees in five large state agencies whose departments were being merged into one overarching umbrella agency were surveyed regarding their perceived job security (outcome expectancy), their self-efficacy for adapting to the organizational transition (self-efficacy judgment), and a number of behavioral and affective outcomes.

## METHOD

### Participants

Participants were drawn from five state government agencies involved in providing human services to the public that were to be merged in an effort to consolidate their operations and reduce redundancy and duplication of services. A task force was appointed to design and implement the merger and agency employees were gradually notified about how these changes were going to affect them. For some employees, the changes would be minimal. For others, the restructuring would involve moving offices, changing supervisors, being demoted, learning new job-related technologies, a reduction in job status, and/or new work tasks. Layoffs had not been specifically mentioned during the announcement of the merger. However, rumors were rampant that they would occur. Consequently, within the same agency, some employees were in danger of losing key features of their job, their current position, or employment with the state, whereas others remained essentially unaffected by the reorganization.

A stratified random sample of 500 employees from these agencies was selected. The basis of stratification was the employee's objective level of job security as judged by the assistant to the director of each agency. In addition, individuals were selected from all levels within the organizational hierarchy. Surveys were administered in-person at each data site where 10 or more individuals had been sampled. Any sites with fewer than 10 sampled individuals were mailed the surveys. A total of 283 individuals responded to the survey – a response rate of 57%. However, a turnover and retirement rate of 9.6% since time of initial sampling resulted in an effective response rate of 63%. Examination of sample demographics did not reveal significant departures from the overall makeup of the organization's workforce suggesting the sample is representative of the organization from which it was selected.

Data were collected from this sample approximately 6 months into the reorganization. During this time, many changes had begun to take effect; however, there was still much uncertainty regarding possible future layoffs, changing policies, changing job technology, etc.

## Measures

A survey assessing the constructs of interest was administered six months into the reorganization. The scales are described below.

### Job Security

The Job Security Index (Probst, 1998; 2001) was used to measure employees' cognitive appraisal of the future of their job with respect to the perceived level of stability and continuance of that job. This was the measure of outcome expectancy. Previous studies using the JSI have found the scale to be extremely reliable (Probst, 2000; 2002; 2003) with Cronbach alpha coefficients consistently above .90.

Respondents indicate on a 3-point scale (yes, ?, no) the extent to which 18 adjectives or phrases described the future of their job (e.g., 'my job is almost guaranteed', 'permanent position if I want it', 'insecure', 'future is vague', 'well-established'). Responses are scored such that higher numbers reflect more job security.

### Self-Efficacy

There is currently no scale that specifically measures self-efficacy for adapting to organizational transitions. Therefore, nine items were written to measure this construct. Respondents were asked to indicate (using a 7-point response scale) the extent to which they agree or disagree with each of the nine statements. Items were written to measure the degree to which an individual feels capable of dealing with general organizational changes as well as specific changes such as new policies, new coworkers, new supervisors, or new responsibilities. A sample item is, 'I feel unsure about my ability to adapt to changes occurring within this agency.'

### Job Satisfaction

The Job Descriptive Index (JDI; Smith, Kendall, and Hulin, 1969), as revised by Roznowski (1989), was used to measure satisfaction with coworkers, pay and promotions, supervision, and the work itself. Respondents indicated using the 3-point (yes, ?, no) response scale the extent to which each adjective or phrase described that aspect of their job. The following are sample items: coworker satisfaction – 'work well together,' pay satisfaction – 'less than I deserve,' promotions satisfaction – 'unfair promotion policy,' supervision satisfaction – 'gives confusing directions,' and work satisfaction – 'gives sense of accomplishment.' Items are scored such that larger numbers indicate more job satisfaction.

### Job Security Satisfaction

Whereas the Job Security Index was designed to assess perceptions of job security, the Job Security Satisfaction scale (JSS; Probst, 1998, 2003) was designed for this study to capture an individual's attitudes regarding that level of job security. The scale consists of a series of adjectives or short phrases describing the various evaluative responses one might have to a perceived level of job security. Although the evaluative response was targeted, 20 adjectives or short phrases such as 'sufficient amount of security,' 'unacceptably low,' and 'makes me anxious' were chosen to span the descriptive-evaluative continuum in the attempt to avoid any general affectivity bias. The response format is identical to that of the JSI.

### Affective Reactions to the Workplace Reorganization

In order to assess affective reactions to the organizational restructuring, individuals were asked to rate on a 5-point scale the extent to which they experienced nine emotions as a result of the workplace reorganization. Responses were scaled such that higher scores reflect more negative affective reactions to the organizational restructuring. Sample emotions assessed were anger, alarm, sadness, happiness, and contentment. These were chosen based on the typology of emotions presented in Shaver, Schwartz, Kirson, and O'Conner (1989).

### Organizational Commitment

The nine-item Organizational Commitment Questionnaire (OCQ) developed by Mowday, Steers, and Porter (1979) measures the relative strength of an individual's identification with and involvement in a particular organization. Using a seven-point response scale, respondents indicated the extent to which they agreed or disagreed with statements such as 'I tell my friends the agency I work for is great.'

### Physical Health

Physical health of respondents was measured using Hanisch's (1992) Health Conditions Index. This scale lists 12 health conditions such as severe headaches and high blood pressure and asks respondents to indicate whether or not they experience the condition using a simple yes/no checklist response format. Responses are scored such that higher numbers indicate the experience of more physical health complaints.

### Job Withdrawal

Job withdrawal was measured using 4 items assessing turnover intentions developed by Hanisch and Hulin (1990, 1991). These items assess respondents' reported desirability and likelihood of quitting. Higher numbers indicate more turnover intentions.

### Work Withdrawal

Eleven work withdrawal items developed by Hanisch and Hulin (1990, 1991) measured reported behavioral attempts to avoid completion of specific work tasks (e.g., missing meetings, being late for work, and work task avoidance). Higher numbers indicate a greater incidence of work withdrawal behaviors.

# RESULTS

The multivariate F statistics indicated self-efficacy for adapting to organizational transitions had significant main effects, $F(7, 255) = 6.48$, $p < .001$, and, with perceptions of job security, significant interactive effects, $F(7,255) = 2.88$, $p < .01$, on the dependent variables of interest. In addition, as has been found in previous research, there were several significant main effects of job insecurity, $F(7,255) = 44.73$, $p < .001$. A summary of the significant univariate F statistics follows.

## Job Security Satisfaction

Self-efficacy for adapting to organizational transitions did not interact with job security perceptions to influence job security satisfaction, $F(1, 261) = .75$, n.s. Rather, self-efficacy had a main effect on the dependent variable, $F(1, 261) = 4.13$, $p < .05$, such that greater self-efficacy was related to more job security satisfaction, supporting Hypothesis 1. In addition, as predicted by Hypothesis 2, there was a significant main effect of job security perceptions on job security satisfaction, $F(1, 229) = 276.12$, $p < .001$, such that greater perceived job security was related to more satisfaction.

## Job Satisfaction

In support of Hypothesis 1, self-efficacy was significantly related to job satisfaction, such that higher self-efficacy was related to greater job satisfaction, $F(1, 261) = 12.42$, $p < .001$. In addition, job security had a main effect on overall job satisfaction, providing support for Hypothesis 2, $F(1, 261) = 10.53$, $p < .001$. There was no significant interaction pattern, $F(1, 261) = 1.37$, n.s.

## Affective Reactions to Organizational Transition

Self-efficacy had a main effect on the affective reactions individuals had to the workplace reorganization, $F(1, 261) = 10.13$, $p < .01$, such that high self-efficacy individuals had fewer negative affective reactions than low self-efficacy individuals. In addition, greater job insecurity was related to more negative affective reactions, $F(1, 261) = 45.45$, $p < .001$. In support of Hypothesis 3, there was a significant interaction between self-efficacy and perceived job security, $F(1, 261) = 4.02$, $p < .05$. To illustrate the nature of the interaction, a median split was performed on the job security and self-efficacy variables and the means were plotted. As can be seen in Figure 1, high self-efficacy appears to buffer the effect of low job security. Although low job security is related to more negative affective reactions, this effect is attenuated among those with high self-efficacy expectancies.

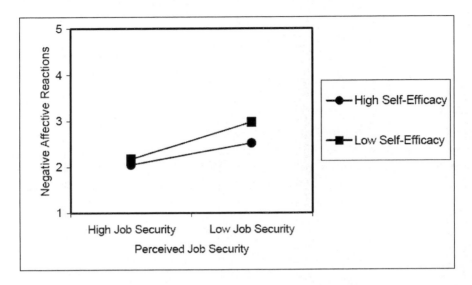

Figure 1. Interactive effects of job insecurity and self-efficacy judgments on negative affective reactions to the organizational transition.

## Organizational Commitment

In support of Hypotheses 1 and 2, main effects were found for self-efficacy, $F(1, 261) = 25.16$, $p < .001$, and for job security, $F(1, 261) = 8.65$, $p < .01$, on employee organizational commitment, such that greater self-efficacy and greater perceived job security were related to higher levels of reported organizational commitment.

Of greater interest, a significant interaction between self-efficacy and job security perceptions was also found for organizational commitment, $F(1, 261) = 5.02$, $p < .05$, supporting Hypothesis 3 . As shown in Figure 2, organizational commitment for individuals with low self-efficacy did not significantly different as a function of their perceived job security. However, among individuals with high self-efficacy for adapting to organizational transitions, organizational commitment was high only when outcome expectancies were high (i.e., job security was high). When job security was low, organizational commitment was more similar to that of individuals with low self-efficacy. Thus, it appears high self-efficacy individuals are more committed to the organization than low self-efficacy individuals when perceived job security is high, but commitment levels of high self-efficacy individuals drops to that of low self-efficacy individuals when perceptions of job security are low.

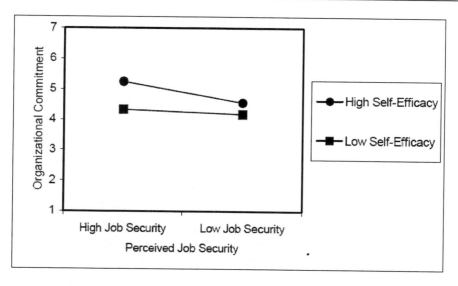

Figure 2. Interactive effects of job insecurity and self-efficacy judgments on organizational commitment.

## Health Conditions

In support of Hypotheses 1 and 2, main effects were found for self-efficacy, $F(1, 261) =$ 4.16, $p < .05$, and for job security, $F(1, 261) = 9.39$, $p < .005$, on employee health conditions, such that greater self-efficacy and greater perceived job security were related to fewer reports of health complaints.

In addition, the interaction between self-efficacy and job security perceptions on health conditions was also significant, $F(1, 261) = 4.25$, $p < .05$, such that individuals with low self-efficacy did not experience a change in their reported health conditions as a function of their perceived job security. However, individuals with high self-efficacy reported more health conditions when job security was perceived to be low than when security was perceived to be high. See Figure 3 for an illustration of the interaction pattern.

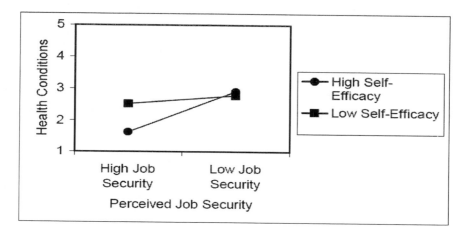

Figure 3. Interactive effects of job insecurity and self-efficacy judgments on physical health conditions.

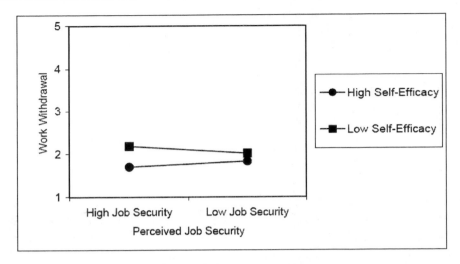

Figure 4. Interactive effects of job insecurity and self-efficacy judgments on work withdrawal behaviors.

## Job Withdrawal

The interaction between self-efficacy and job security perceptions for turnover intentions was non-significant, $F(1, 261) = .03$, n.s. In addition, the main effect for job security perceptions on turnover intentions was also non-significant, $F(1, 261) = .2.25$, n.s. However, there was a main effect for self-efficacy, higher self-efficacy was related to fewer turnover intentions, $F(1, 261) = 14.77$, $p < .001$.

## Work Withdrawal

Analysis of work withdrawal behaviors resulted in similar findings, such that higher self-efficacy was related to a lower incidence of work withdrawal behaviors, $F(1, 261) = .23.25$, $p < .001$. In addition, there was also a marginally significant interaction between self-efficacy and job security perceptions, $F(1, 261) = 3.12$, $p < .08$, such that low self-efficacy individuals engaged in more work withdrawal behaviors than high self-efficacy individuals under conditions of high job security. When perceptions of job security were low, there was little difference between the reported work withdrawal behaviors of the two groups.

## CONCLUSION

The purpose of this study was to examine the extent to which self-efficacy for adapting to organizational transitions would buffer the negative effects of job insecurity. Based on the theory of self-efficacy, it was predicted that self-efficacy would be related to more positive job-related outcomes. However, it was anticipated that self-efficacy would serve to buffer the stress of working in an organization undergoing a major transition primarily when the employee's outcome expectancy (i.e., job security) was also positive.

As anticipated , self-efficacy for adapting to organizational transitions was related to a number of positive work outcomes. Individuals who scored higher on the self-efficacy for adapting to organizational transitions scale were more satisfied with their jobs than individuals who rated themselves as less capable of adapting to organizational transitions. High self-efficacy individuals also reported fewer negative affective reactions to the workplace reorganization, greater organizational commitment, fewer turnover intentions, and less frequent work withdrawal behaviors. Finally, high self-efficacy employees also reported fewer physical health complaints than low self-efficacy employees.

However, the main effects do not tell the entire story. When job security was perceived to be high, high self-efficacy employees reported more organizational commitment, fewer health conditions, and fewer work withdrawal behaviors than individuals with low self-efficacy. When job security was perceived to be low, commitment, heath, and work withdrawal behaviors were not significantly different from those of low self-efficacy employees. In each case, this was due to high self-efficacy employees being adversely affected by the perception of insecurity.

What might explain the repeated finding that, overall, individuals with high self-efficacy exhibit attractive employee qualities, but that these employees are more negatively affected by the introduction of insecurity into the workplace? According to Kanfer and Ackerman (1989), there is a set amount of available cognitive resources that each individual has when engaged in the completion of any given task. On-task, off-task, and self-regulatory activities compete for these cognitive resources. When individuals have high self-efficacy for attaining a goal (e.g., adapting to organizational transitions) and goal-performance discrepancies are small (i.e., high job security), self-regulatory activities are disengaged, leaving more resources available for the on- and off-task activities. Possibly, when job security is high, individuals with high self-efficacy have more positive outcomes than individuals with low self-efficacy, because they have more resources available to expend towards those activities. However, when job security is perceived to be low (i.e., large discrepancies between goal and performance), some of those excess cognitive resources are funneled into self-regulatory activities aimed at monitoring progress towards the goal. Thus, possibly low self-efficacy individuals engage in more self-regulatory activities that expend valuable cognitive resources (Bandura and Cervone, 1986; Kanfer and Ackerman, 1989), whereas high self-efficacy individuals do not utilize these resources unless a threat is perceived, i.e., during times of insecurity.

This explanation comports with Bandura's (1982) assertion that both outcome expectancies and self-efficacy expectancies need to be high for positive outcomes to occur. When job security is high, outcome expectancies are high. In this situation, high self-efficacy would be expected to be related to positive outcomes. However, when job security is low, and outcome expectancies are reduced, outcomes are not expected to be as positive. Finally, when self-efficacy is low, outcome expectancies play a lesser role, because outcomes are not predicted to be positive except under conditions of positive self-efficacy expectations.

The results of this study suggest that self-efficacy for adapting to organizational transitions does play an important role in buffering individuals during times of organizational change. Although high self-efficacy does not relieve employees of the stresses associated with organizational change when they perceive their job security to be threatened, more positive outcomes are noted when the employee's job security is assessed to be positive. This implies that it is extremely important for an organization to accurately communicate to employees the extent to which their jobs will be affected by any pending organizational transitions. Employees with high self-efficacy can be expected to fare well during times of transition, but only if they know that their jobs are not at risk. Oftentimes, organizational communication declines during times of change. This reduction of communication can unnecessarily put high self-efficacy employees at risk by channeling their cognitive efforts away from work tasks and towards off-task activities, such as coping with the perceived threat of job loss – regardless of whether that threat is factual or not.

# REFERENCES

Ashford, S., Lee, C., and Bobko, P. (1989). Content, causes, and consequences of job insecurity: A theory-based measure and substantive test. *Academy of Management Journal*, 32, 803-829.

Bandura, A. (1982). Self-efficacy mechanism in human agency. *American Psychologist*, 37, 122-147.

Bandura, A., and Cervone, D. (1986). Differential engagement of self-reactive influences in cognitive motivation. *Organizational Behavior and Human Decision Processes*, 38, 92-113.

Bandura, A., and Schunk, D. H. (1981). Cultivating competence, self-efficacy, and intrinsic interest through proximal self-motivation. *Journal of Personality and Social Psychology*, 41, 586-598.

Beck, A.T. (1976). *Cognitive therapy and the emotional disorders*. New York: International Universities Press.

Brenner, S., Arnetz, B., Levi, L., Hall, E., Hjelm, R., Petterson, I., Salovarra, H., Soerbom, D., Tellenback, S., and Akerstedt, T. (December, 1983). *The effects of insecurity at work, job loss, and unemployment: Project description and preliminary findings*. Paper presented at the WHO conference on unemployment and health, Stockholm.

Buessing, A. (1986). Worker responses to job insecurity: A quasi-experimental field investigation. In G. Debus and H.W. Schroiff (Eds.), *The Psychology of Work and Organization*. (p. 137-144). North Holland: Elsevier Science Publishers.

Cottington, E. M., Matthews, K. A., Talbot, E., et al. (1986). Occupational stress, suppressed anger, and hypertension. *Psychosomatic Medicine*, 48, 249-260.

Davy, J., Kinicki, A., and Scheck, C. (1991). Developing and testing a model of survivor responses to layoffs. *Journal of Vocational Behavior*, 38, 302-317.

Dekker, S. W., and Schaufeli, W. B. (1995). The effects of job insecurity on psychological health and withdrawal: A longitudinal study. *Australian Psychologist*, 30, 57-63.

Dooley, D., Rook, K., and Catalano, R. (1987). Job and non-job stressors and their moderators. *Journal of Occupational Psychology*, 60, 115-132.

Greenhalgh, L. and Rosenblatt, Z. (1984). Job insecurity: Towards conceptual clarity. *Academy of Management Review*, 9, 438-448.

Hanisch, K.A. (1992). *The development of a Health Condition scale and its relations to health satisfaction and retirement valence*. Paper presented at the 2nd APA/NIOSH Conference on Stress and the Workplace. Washington, D.C.: November.

Hanisch, K. A., and Hulin, C. L. (1990). Job attitudes and organizational withdrawal: An examination of retirement and other voluntary withdrawal behaviors. *Journal of Vocational Behavior,* 37, 60-78.

Hanisch, K. A., and Hulin, C. L. (1991). General attitudes and organizational withdrawal: An evaluation of a causal model. *Journal of Vocational Behavior,* 39, 110-128.

Kanfer, R., and Ackerman, P. L. (1989). Motivation and cognitive abilities: An integrative/aptitude-treatment interaction approach to skill acquisition. *Journal of Applied Psychology,* 74(4), 657-690.

Kuhnert, K., Sims, R., and Lahey, M. (1989). The relationship between job security and employees health. *Group and Organization Studies,* 14, 399-410.

Lazarus, R.S., and Launier, R. (1978). Stress-related transactions between person and environment. In L.A. Pervin and M. Lewis (Eds.) *Perspectives in interactional psychology.* New York: Plenum Press.

Mowday, R., Steers, R., and Porter, L. (1979). The measurement of organizational commitment. *Journal of Vocational Behavior,* 14, 224-247.

Probst, T. M. (1998). *Antecedents and consequences of job security: Development and test of an integrated model.* Unpublished doctoral dissertation. University of Illinois at Urbana-Champaign.

Probst, T.M. (2000). Wedded to the job: Moderating effects of job involvement on the consequences of job insecurity. *Journal of Occupational Health Psychology,* 5, 63-73.

Probst, T.M. (2003). Development and validation of the Job Security Index and the Job Security Satisfaction Scale: A classical test theory and IRT approach. *Journal of Occupational and Organizational Psychology,* 76, 451-467.

Probst, T.M. (2002). The impact of job insecurity on employee work attitudes, job adaptation, and organizational withdrawal behaviors. In J. M. Brett and F. Drasgow (Eds.) *The psychology of work: Theoretically based empirical research.* (pp. 141-168). New Jersey: Lawrence Erlbaum Associates.

Probst, T.M. and Brubaker, T.L. (2001). The effects of job insecurity on employee safety outcomes: Cross-sectional and longitudinal explorations. *Journal of Occupational Health Psychology,* 6, 139-159.

Roskies, E. and Louis-Guerin, C. (1990). Job insecurity in managers: Antecedents and consequences. *Journal of Organizational Behavior,* 11, 345-359.

Sherer, M., Maddux, J. E., Mercadante, B., Prentice-Dunn, S., and Rogers, R. W. (1982). The self-efficacy scale: Construction and validation. *Psychological Reports,* 51, 663-671.

Simons, J. (1998, November 18). Despite low unemployment, layoffs soar – corporate mergers and overseas turmoil are cited as causes. *The Wall Street Journal,* p. A2.

Smith, P.C., Kendall, L., and Hulin, C.L. (1969). *The measurement of satisfaction in work and retirement.* Chicago: Rand McNally.

In: Industrial Psychology Research Trends
Editor: Ina M. Pearle, pp. 23-45

ISBN: 978-1-60021-825-5
© 2007 Nova Science Publishers, Inc.

*Chapter 2*

# PROTECTING THE TURF THAT'S WORTH PROTECTING: MEDICAL RESISTANCE TO 'MID-LEVEL' HEALTH CARE PROVIDERS

## *Sally Lindsay*[*]

Institute for Social, Cultural and Policy Research;
University of Salford, Salford, United Kingdom; M5 4QA

## ABSTRACT

Despite the increased use of mid-level health care providers in an effort to save money and fill gaps in physician shortages there has been little examination of their experience of medical resistance. Examining this is important because the extent of collaboration can influence job satisfaction, retention, inter-professional relations and patient care. This study explored the extent to which mid-level providers experienced medical resistance though qualitative semi-structured interviews with 59 health care providers (nurse practitioners (NPs), nurse anesthetists (CRNAs), physician assistants (PAs) and key informants). The results suggest that the amount of resistance varied by gender, type of provider and the extent of 'substitutability.' Jurisdictional disputes seemed most evident around the areas that were most valued by physicians, while there was less resistance around the fringes. Key tensions arose around financial concerns and maintaining medical dominance, while some physicians resisted because they lacked knowledge of the role. Mid-level providers experienced resistance from both the political level and in day-to-day practice. Each of the providers varied in the extent to which they considered themselves a substitute provider. CRNAs saw themselves as substitute providers more often than a complement, while NPs were somewhat mixed. Meanwhile, PAs viewed themselves as a complement provider more often than a substitute. Those who considered themselves a 'complementary' provider reported less resistance compared to those who considered themselves a substitute. There were three key areas where physicians did not put up as much resistance towards mid-level providers: devalued tasks, less desirable patient groups and devalued geographical locations. In

[*] Sally Lindsay: Email: s.lindsay@salford.ac.uk

conclusion, the extent of resistance experienced by mid-level providers varied by the extent of 'substitutability' of the provider and also by gender.

**Keywords:** mid-level providers, medical resistance, medical dominance, inter-professional relations.

# INTRODUCTION

Given that the health care industry is labour-intensive, reforms have a profound effect on the structure and organization of the health care division of labour (Armstrong and Armstrong 2003). Hospitals and other health agencies have begun to analyze the efficiency of their operations and skill mix of their employees in efforts to save money. One common cost saving measure is the substitution of less expensive workers for more costly physician providers (Auerbach 2000). This changes the structure of professional boundaries and influences inter-professional dynamics. Most research focuses on the cost-effectiveness of such providers and physicians' and clients' views of them, yet little is known about the experiences of mid-level providers and how professional dynamics are shaped by their presence. Examining medical resistance is salient because the extent of collaboration can influence patient care and job satisfaction (Amost and Lascinger 2002).

## Who Are Mid-Level Providers?

Mid-level providers, also commonly known as non-physician clinicians or substitute providers are increasingly offering health care that has traditionally been provided by physicians. Given that the growth of mid-level providers is expected to increase by 150% in the U.S. over the next decade it is relevant to examine how professional boundaries are being affected (Cooper et al. 1998b). There are several reasons for the increased use of mid-level providers' including: increased growth in such providers, changes in state laws and regulations expanding the practice prerogatives of these providers and their autonomy from physician supervision,' and payers have increased their access to reimbursement (Cooper 2001). Thus, many providers are undertaking tasks previously provided by physicians. The consequence of this shift in providers is that it reshapes the division of labor, altering traditional professional boundaries.

The numbers of mid-level providers graduating in the U.S. doubled between 1992 and 1997. Along with the growth in mid-level providers, the breadth of clinical responsibility has been expanding as their scope of practice increases (Cooper 2001). This chapter examines nurse practitioners, physician assistants and nurse anesthetists because they comprise an increasing proportion of the labor force and offer a range of the varying ways that they can complement or substitute for physicians (Bureau of Health Professions 2000).

In the U.S. mid-level providers can perform up to eighty percent of the same tasks as physicians for a fraction of the cost (AANA 2003). Nurse practitioners (NPs) are registered nurses who have additional training that enables them to diagnose and manage most common illnesses, either independently or as part of a team (ACNP 2006). Training for NPs is through either a certificate or a master's degree where they focus on health maintenance, disease prevention, counseling and patient education (ACNP 2006). NPs are the largest group of traditional mid-level providers and this group has undergone the most rapid growth. The number of NPs has increased over the last 10 years from approximately 30,000 to 65,000 (Cooper 2001).

Physician assistants (PAs) in the U.S. are health professionals who are licensed to practice medicine under physician supervision. They make clinical decisions and provide a broad range of diagnostic, therapeutic, preventive and health maintenance services (AAPA 2003). Unlike nursing-based disciplines PAs grew out of a medical tradition and their training is in the context of collaborative care directed by physicians (Cooper et al. 1998a). Although PAs are limited to practicing with physician direction, that supervision may be intermittent and at a distance. Thus, the actual autonomy of PAs may be substantial (Cooper 2001).

Finally, nurse anesthetists (CRNAs) in the U.S. are registered nurses who have additional training and administer anesthesia, monitor patient's vital signs during surgery and provide post-anesthesia care (Bureau of Labor Statistics 2006). They administer approximately 65% of all anesthetics given in the U.S. each year (AANA 2003). Next, reasons why there has been an increase in the use of mid-level providers in recent years is discussed.

## Why Is There an Increase in Mid-Level Providers?

Efforts to reduce health care spending in the U.S. have led to the increased use of 'mid-level' health care providers (Deuben 1998). For example, health economists estimate that up to $8.75 billion could be saved annually if NPs were used more extensively since their salary is about three and a half times less than physicians' (Calpin-Davies and Akehurst 1999). PAs are also proposed as a cost-effective solution to America's health care crisis in that they can free doctors' time to treat more complicated patients (AAPA 2003). There are also significant cost savings in using CRNAs, who make on average $84,000, compared to anaesthesiologists who make an average of $244,000 per year (AANA 2003).

Changes in state laws have also enhanced the practice of non-physician providers. Thus, the market has created new opportunities for mid-level providers to engage in clinical practice (Cooper et al. 2001). In 1977 the Rural Health Clinics Act provided reimbursement for NPs and PAs; however, it was limited to those working in health profession shortage areas. This was expanded in the Balanced Budget Act of 1997 to include other locations and onsite physician supervision was also waived unless it was a requirement of the state (Cooper et al. 2001). A similar change affecting CRNAs was adopted in 2000.

## Impact on Physicians

The increased presence of substitute providers has had a notable impact on physicians. Throughout most of the twentieth century, physicians have maintained a dominant position in the health care division of labor through the control over content, terms and conditions of its work, control over clients and other health professions (Friedson 1988). Physicians held a virtual monopoly over other providers for decades where their dominance was established through state licensure and regulation, third party reimbursement and a rise in the number of physicians (Cooper et al. 1998b). More recently, this dominance is increasingly being challenged with the creation of non-physician providers (Grumbach and Coffman 1998). Physicians often view themselves in competition with mid-level providers and are often reluctant to support their increased use because many are concerned about their jurisdiction (Martin and Hutchinson 1999).

Much of the literature examines the extent to which mid-level providers are seen as competition (Auerbach 2000; Birenbaum 1994; Mundinger 1994). Some find that physicians who work with mid-levels are generally supportive of the role (Aquilino 1999), while others claim that greater familiarity of the role is needed to promote collaboration between physicians and NPs (Macay 2003; MacDonald and Katz 2002). Johnson and Freeborn (1986) found that physicians' attitudes towards NPs were less favorable than their attitudes towards PAs. This was largely a result of NPs wanting more independence whereas PAs are more complementary to physicians. The quality of care and patient satisfaction for mid-level providers is similar to physicians (Laurant et al. 2006). Much of the literature has focused on the impact of mid-level providers on physicians while much less is known about how and the extent to which they encounter medical resistance.

## Mid-Level Provider's Experience

Non-physician providers are also concerned about the nature and degree of overlap with physicians, yet there has been much less examination of mid-level provider's experience (Drus et al. 2003). Several common themes exist in terms of where they practice. Mid-level providers are more likely to care for under-served and vulnerable populations than primary care physicians (Grumbach et al. 2003; Mittman et al. 2002). For example, there are a higher proportion of mid-level providers in primary care because it arguably 'holds relatively little allure' for physicians since specialists are often better paid and have more prestige among their colleagues (Cesa and Larente 2004). Large proportions of mid-level providers also practice in rural communities, in communities with high proportions of low-income residents and in health professions shortage areas (Grumbach et al. 2003). In Bankert's (1989) account of the nurse anesthesia profession she captures similar sentiments of a nurse anesthetist:

> I'd only been out of school a short time and already I'd learned that nurse anesthetists were considered incompetent in places like Denver or San Francisco, but completely qualified to do anything and everything in the inner city slums or isolated small towns...Our competence is also related to the setting and the rising of the sun.

Mid-level providers also tend to perform tasks involving lower-complexity and provide more health advice and achieve higher levels of patient satisfaction compared with doctors (Cooper 2001; Laurant et al. 2006).

This inter-professional conflict is further complicated by traditional physician-nurse relationships which are characterized by a pattern of physician dominance and nurse deference (Torgersen and Chamings 1994). It is often difficult for nurses to 'shed the handmaiden to the physician' role to gain more autonomy and power (Torgersen and Chamings 1994). For example, Cohen et al. (1998) found that most NPs expressed concerns of being 'invisible' providers and felt that their services were not recognized as being major contributing factors to the overall services that were provided.

GPs often favorably view NP functions traditionally associated with nursing (teaching, history taking) but less favorably to functions associated with medicine (prescribing, ordering tests and physical assessment) (Mackay 2003). In sum, there has been little examination of mid-level provider's experience of medical resistance. Most research focuses on their cost-effectiveness, productivity and physicians' views of them.

## Theoretical Perspectives: Medical Dominance and Professional Jurisdiction

Until recently, the medical profession has maintained its autonomy and dominance over the health care division of labour and resource allocation. Freidson (1970) outlined this notion in his medical dominance thesis, which refers to the way in which a profession uses legal and clinical autonomy to gain control over competing professional groups, over the profession's institutional domain, and over its financing. Achieving medical dominance involved two stages. The first stage included demonstrating that the occupation does reliable and valuable work. The emergence of scientific medicine also helped to achieve a monopoly in the health care division of labour. The second stage involved the conferral of autonomy, which results from the interaction of political and economic power (Friedson 1970). Physicians gained dominance by using their contacts with the state and elite class to help pass legislation that exerted their influence and suppressed irregular healers. The medical profession dominated the medical care system in the production of medical knowledge, the health care division of labor, and the organization of medicine (Freidson 1970).

Although there is disagreement over the extent to which medical dominance is declining, most researchers agree on its numerous causes. First, medical dominance is declining because of increased state involvement, which is largely a result of efforts to make health care more efficient and profitable. The state's rationalizing of health care and call for greater competition, deregulation and privatization are limiting doctor's autonomy and dominance (Conrad 1992). Managed care is the major force in deconstructing professional autonomy since management emphasizes accountability and efficiency through monitoring and control. Indeed, the restructuring of the health care division of labour may weaken physicians' control over their work as mid-level health care providers are able to conduct their work outside of doctor's control (Hafferty and Light 1995).

Physicians are also facing challenges from other health professions, who are questioning their authority, expertise and the scientific validity of medicine (Armstrong and Armstrong 2003). With health reforms and the increasing encroachment of other health professions on medicine's territory, physicians are now required to work as a team, which flattens the hierarchical division of labor.

Second, there is increasing pressure from new professionals to take over and encroach upon the domain of the most established professions within the medical field. Turner (1995) argues that professions are subject to external forces, which fragment and subordinate their activities to the interests of capital. The capacity to withstand deskilling will be a consequence of the cohesion of professional groups, their level of state support, and their location within the hierarchy of professional skills (Turner 1995). With the encroachment of new health care providers, traditional professional boundaries are blurring and may intensify the debate over provider roles.

## Professional Jurisdiction

The decline of medical dominance and the accompanying increase of mid-level providers alters professional jurisdiction within the health care division of labour. Abbott's (1988) concept of jurisdiction refers to an area of knowledge or expertise that comprises an interdependent structural network, which he referred to as 'the system of professions.' Within this notion, professions are seen to develop inter-relations with other professions when an existing jurisdiction becomes available or when a new one is created (Abbott 1988). Jurisdiction is influenced by external systems such as changes in working conditions, public opinion and administration. The success in a profession occupying a jurisdiction depends on the situation of its competitors as much as their own efforts. It is important to use a systems approach because it takes inter-professional competition into account.

Abbott (1988) sees jurisdictional disputes or struggles for control over areas of work as key events among professions. Such conflicts occur when social forces create or diminish work domains and when one profession tries to encroach upon an occupied arena. Professional power theories suggest that jurisdictional dominance varies with the extent of physicians' hold over subordinates occupational structures. Abbott argues that most jurisdictional struggles occur in the workplace, public opinion and legal/administrative rule. Conflicts over boundaries can result in split jurisdiction or the subordination of one profession by another (Halpern 1992). Halpern argues that the dynamics among a profession's internal segments are critical in shaping its cross-professional boundaries.

Substitution, also referred to as encroachment (Germov 1998) draws on the Neo-Weberian concept of social closure which acknowledges the exclusionary and usurpationary strategies aimed at boundary encroachment or maintenance (Eaton and Webb 1979). In many cases substitution may also arise from the active discarding of unwanted tasks, or 'ditching the dirty work' to another provider (Hughes 1958; Hugman 1991; Nancarrow and Borthick 2005). This refers to those with high professional standing retaining the most desirable work delegating the less pleasant work to others with less standing. Women often perform the majority of such tasks because they lack power and access to resources to obtain higher paying and higher status positions (Butter et al. 1994). It may also be a result of the physician-nurse relationship being characterized by a pattern of physician dominance and nurse submission with increasing conflict between the two (Torgersen and Chamings 1994).

## METHODS

The objective of this chapter is to explore the extent to which mid-level providers experience medical resistance. To examine this, qualitative semi-structured interviews were conducted with 59 health care providers and key informants knowledgeable about the each of the professions (such as presidents of PA, CRNA and NP associations and deans of such schools) were conducted in New York State and Pennsylvania, U.S. (refer to table 1). These locations were chosen because they provide examples of high utilizations of mid-level providers (AANA 2003; Bureau of Health Professions 2000). A mix of rural and urban sites was used to capture the range of substitutability in these providers.

**Table 1. Overview of Interviews**

| OCCUPATION | Study Sites | Total |
|---|---|---|
| Nurse practitioners | New York | 12 |
| Key informants | | 6 |
| Physician assistants | New York | 15 |
| Key informants | | 6 |
| Nurse anesthetists | Pennsylvania | 15 |
| Key informants | | 5 |
| | | Total 59 |

Telephone interviews were conducted from August 2003 to January 2004 and lasted between thirty and ninety minutes. Health providers were identified through college and health association registries and relevant Internet sites. Potential informants were contacted by phone or email and the objectives of the study were conveyed along with the project information form. A date and time for a follow-up phone call was then established.

The interview schedule had core questions with probes to allow for comparisons to be made between the interviews. Health care providers were asked to describe their work, any experiences of medical resistance and the extent to which the felt they were a complement or substitute provider. Key informants were asked to describe the resistance felt at the legislative level. All interviews were tape-recorded and transcribed verbatim.

Data collected through interviews were sorted, coded and categorized according to emergent themes with the aid of NVIVO, a qualitative data analysis software program (Richards 1999). Similarities and differences between each of the provider groups and gender were examined. This research used an unfolding paradigm with general guiding questions and a oosely structured design so that categories and codes can emerge from the data, during analysis aposterioi. Through inductive analysis, patterns and themes were identified around resistance, devalued work, and whether they considered themselves a substitute or complement provider. Here "resistance" is referred to an action of opposing something that you disagree with (Oxford Dictionary 2006). This program assisted in condensing the data and identifying relationships among central themes around the issues of medical resistance, and devalued work. The method for this project drew on interpretive traditions within qualitative research where the researcher seeks an in-depth understanding of the experiences of the participants (Green and Thorogood 2004). The analysis began by reading through each transcript several times and noting emerging themes and patterns. Analysis gradually evolved into the stage of axial coding, which was concerned with the properties of the themes and their inter-relationships. This study received approval from a university research ethics board.

Frequency tables were calculated based on the number of examples of resistance and devalued labor that each of the providers experienced. Respondents were also asked whether they considered themselves a "complement" or "substitute" provider and this was also categorized by type of health care provider and gender. A similar table was also constructed for key informants.

# RESULTS

The results suggest several common views of how providers experience resistance. First, insight from the mid-level provider's view is provided as to why physicians are resisting. Then, how physicians resist at both the political level and in day-to-day practice is discussed. Third, the provider's views of the extent of their substitutability or complementary nature are examined. Finally, the areas of least resistance are explored and include devalued tasks, less desirable patient groups, specialty areas, and devalued geographical locations.

## Why Physicians Are Resisting

Several common views across the three different provider groups arose offering insight into why physicians resist and included issues around liability, maintenance of medical dominance, cost, and lack of knowledge about the role. Many of the mid-level providers said that physicians were concerned about the potential liability of hiring NPs and PAs. For example,

> The physician said prior to her coming on she had discussions with the medical association and she said they *put the fear of God into you* about working with an NP. That's how the medical association is approaching it. So the question is how do we get to the medical association and educate them? For whatever reason, they may see us as a threat. I don't know. I think they don't understand the role completely. Whether that's by choice, or by improper education. They feel that, and this is through her, she was told that 'do you know that you're putting your license on the line if you're working with a nurse practitioner and what happens if there's a mistake?' and that kind of thing. (Female NP #1)

Such views are often supported by medical associations and reinforce medical dominance over the health care division of labour. Many of the providers felt that

> The medical association is somewhat resistive to nurse practitioners and it's just purely a turf issue. I don't really blame them for that. To some degree that's their job to protect their turf as the political arm of the group. But who are they speaking for? In any professional group the people who are actually politically active are a pretty small minority. You know, so it's hard to tell whether it's the majority of the physicians who feel that way or just a small vocal minority. You know, it's hard to say. I think the more exposure there is, the less resistance there is and I think I've seen that over the last few years. But there still is resistance out there in a significant way. (Male NP #3)

Others similarly claimed, "physicians are hanging on to the power that they think they need to hang on to" (Female NP #6)—suggesting that physicians may be reluctant about new professions encroaching on their territory. The encroachment of mid-level providers on to physicians' territory has led them to put up some resistance. For some, this may be a result of a lack of familiarity of the role while others may be tired of the increased encroachment of non-physician providers.

I think there was a lot more hesitation about 'who are these people? How are they trained?' and would it be safe to use them and now that we've gone through a period where there's a lot more acceptance in the last decade? Now that has started to shift a bit to some resistance not so much based on, 'well gee, PAs aren't safe or they don't know what they're doing'; but it's, 'gee they're going to take some of my turf here.' And everybody wants my turf. I think the physicians feel quite put upon by virtually everybody, the pharmDs want to write prescriptions. The chiropractors are trying to expand their practice. There's just a whole host of folks that I guess physicians feel like, boy, this used to be my turf and now everybody wants to play here. (PA key informant #2).

Many of the key informants said that most physicians were opposed to non-physician providers to some extent. For example, they claimed:

physician groups still see this as a turf issue etc., and they're not taking full recognition of the changes in health care delivery system that are happening that are really not going to allow for the kind of traditional practice that we've had either because of cost or because of resource lack. (CRNA key informant #2)

Money is another key issue causing tension between physicians and mid-level providers because they are often seen as taking money out of physicians' pockets. For example, the providers interviewed here said: "If having a nurse practitioner in the area is going to cost them a dime, it's a very negative thing" (Female NP #3). Others reported:

it always boils down to dollars and cents. If physicians feel that you're taking money out of their pocket, it's not going to happen. The PA is only going to be there if you're making money for them. (Male PA #4)

Nurse anesthetists arguably felt this the most as they have historically provided anesthesia much longer than physicians.

For 100 years nurse anesthetists have provided anesthesia care independently in rural areas and in the military and now all of a sudden when you can make a lot of money doing it they [physician anesthesiologists] want to take over. (Male CRNA #2)

Some providers felt that physicians limited their scope of practice so they could bill for a higher amount. For example, a nurse anesthetist claimed "MDs limit what you do so that they can submit higher bills for this, that and the other thing. It's purely money" (Female CRNA #5). Indeed, finances seemed to be a major point of contention:

I think it has to do with turf and funding. There always seems to be this big battle going on between the medical association and the nurse practitioners. The medical association feels that there's a pot of money in the sky and that nobody else should be touching it. (Female NP # 2)

Many providers highlighted that the resistance they encountered might have been a result of physician's lack of knowledge of their role. For example, several claimed something like this: "For whatever reason, they may see us as a threat. I think they don't understand the role completely… There's definitely a knowledge deficit there for some around the role and the scope" (Female NP #1). Others said:

> In my area there are a lot of physicians who don't really understand what nurse practitioners do and what their scope of practice is. That tends to be a point of contention and resistance. I've gotten enough resistance from them that it's endangered the care of patients. (Female NP #4)

It was interesting to note that most physicians who lacked knowledge of or exposure to the role also tended to be older, or had never worked with such a provider. For example,

> The docs that are not in favor of PAs or NPs have usually never worked with them. It's more of a lack of exposure, lack of experience. As there are more PAs and in medical school I know that here all of our medical students by the time they finish they will have been exposed to PAs. Many of them come even into the admissions process thinking I will surely work with PAs and NPs in my future. As it just becomes part of it and increasingly PAs are not just in primary care they're in the teaching centers so it's likely that you'll have run into—every medical student will have worked along side either a PA student or a practicing PA or NP. And that's really how it changes I think. And they think well of course I will have this. I think that's kind of how that works. (PA Key informant #5).

Other PAs noticed "they're just not really aware of what the role is."

> physicians who are worried about PAs taking their turf, encroaching on their territory are ones who have never worked with a PA…For the most part they do tend to be older. (Male PA #7)

Younger physicians seemed to be more familiar with their roles and seemed not to have as many turf issues.

> The younger physicians are more open to it. Some of the older ones are more concerned that we're encroaching on their playing field. I think it's because they're feeling a crunch from every direction. Chiropractors want to do primary care medicine. Nurse practitioners want to hang out their own shingle. You've got all these different groups that are out there. Pharmacists want to run their own clinic. Not to say that these are good or bad things, but with each of them going on it becomes another nick and another nick at their turf. (Male PA #2)

Younger physicians may have a better understanding of mid-level provider's role because they often train alongside mid-level providers. In sum, mid-level providers experienced resistance because physicians wanted to protect their turf and income. Some resistance seemed to result from physician's lack of knowledge about the role.

## How Are Physicians Resisting?

The interviews suggest that mid-level providers experienced resistance at both the political level and in day-to-day practice. The extent of resistance varied by gender and type of provider. Many of the providers discussed how medical associations often put up 'road blocks' to prevent them from gaining more independence. For example, the American Academy of Family Physicians' position is that

> nurse practitioners should not function as an independent health practitioner...the nurse practitioner should only function in an integrated practice arrangement under the direction and responsible supervision of a practicing, licensed physician (AAFP 2006:1).

Their position is stated similarly for PAs. The American Academy of Nurse Practitioners claims that "advanced nurses make independent and collaborative health decisions. They practice autonomously and in collaboration with health care professionals" (AANP 2006). Meanwhile the American Academy of Physician Assistants (2006) claims that PAs are "licensed to practice medicine with physician supervision." These position statements suggest a potential turf conflict between physicians and mid-level providers and possible differences in how they may be treated.

The American Association of Nurse Anesthetists takes the position that they are "qualified independently to perform without supervision by an anesthesiologist or other physician, all the services an anesthesiologist can perform" (AANA 2006). Meanwhile, the American Society of Anesthesiologists takes the position that CRNAs are "qualified to perform some but not all of these services and only under the supervision of a physician" (ASA 2004). This notable difference may contribute to conflicts over boundaries. Several providers and key informants highlighted such tensions at the political level and commented:

> The AMAs #1 objective is the prevention of expansion of any mid-level practitioners. The hope is that as we're working better and better with the medical society that they will realize that, look we're working with you, not against you. But it still comes back to the 'old boy's network,' of hey; hey you're in my backyard. (PA Key Informant #2)

> There are certainly a lot of issues that lend themselves to you seeing that there are biases or road blocks that they still want to put up (Female NP #2)

The CRNAs felt a similar resistance:

> Legislatively it's a daily struggle from session to session. Physician societies in most states whether they're the general medical society or the society of anesthesiologists want to maintain strict control over basically all practice settings and overall advance practice nurses. They feel that advanced practice nurses are reaching well beyond their scope and they want to control it. So anything that goes you have to get their permission, which defeats the purpose of going on to achieving that advance practice status and not being allowed to be using your education. You need to maintain a scope of practice that's fair and equitable and that's appropriate for each practice setting, whether it's a nurse practitioner, midwife or CRNA. (CRNA Key informant # 5)

Many of these 'road blocks' were also felt on a day-to-day basis for several of the providers. They claimed that physicians were often uncomfortable with allowing a non-physician provider to have autonomy.

My position as a PA was challenged routinely by a group of physicians because they weren't comfortable with the idea of somebody without a medical degree practicing and making independent decisions. (Female PA #1)

Physicians want to create legislation that promotes delegation, supervision and believe it or not it's all about the money and power. We're the only competition they have. (Male CRNA #7)

Others felt resistance more at the day-to-day practice level because they were seen as taking their patients. Some claimed that they did not receive the respect that they should have and felt this may have been a result of their position.

When I've made referrals to emerg they haven't dealt with them the way I felt they should have. I said, 'are these doctors in emerge ignoring me because I'm an NP?' (Female NP #1)

The challenges that really cause us the most grief are the turf and financial battles with anesthesiologists. We are probably the nursing specialty that most often goes head-to-head in competition with physicians. Everyday is a battle and has continued. A lot of the issues all circle around autonomy, turf and economic issues. (CRNA key informant #1)

PAs reported less resistance, compared to NPs and CRNAs (refer to table 2), which may have been a result of their close relationship with medicine and their complementary position. Several PAs commented:

Physicians tend to view PAs more favorably than NPs because they have that similar medical model background. I think there are some out there who would see us as trying to get a little piece of their business. But for the most part they see as another set of hands to help them out. (Female PA #4).

We have a very close relationship with the medical society. I think it's because of the medical background and the fact that we want to work complementary with them as opposed to replacing them. The fact that we don't feel we're able to replace them. that we can provide some of the services that they could provide. Certainly we realize that. (Female PA #7)

NP and CRNA key informants reported the most resistance from physicians while PAs had the least (refer to table 3). This may have been a result of PA's close ties with medicine and their more dependent role. The rest of the providers were approximately the same.

In sum, mid-level providers experienced resistance from physicians in several different ways. Most CRNAs and PAs said that their day-to-day inter-professional relations were fine for the most part; however, they felt resistance at the political level. It was interesting to note that PAs experienced less resistance than NPs and CRNAs, which may have been a result of their close ties with medicine. Female providers discussed resistance at more of a personal level while males described it at a political level. This suggests that gender may play a role in mid-level provider's experience as well.

## Table 2. Frequencies of Resistance and Devalued Labor Examples by Provider Type

| | Resistance | | Devalued labor | |
|---|---|---|---|---|
| | Male | Female | Male | Female |
| Nurse practitioners | | | | |
| 1 | 0s | 2s | 2 | 2 |
| 2 | 3c | 2c | 2 | 5 |
| 3 | 1c | 1c | 0 | 4 |
| 4 | 0c | 6s | 0 | 4 |
| 5 | 0c | 7s | 0 | 2 |
| 6 | 2s | 2s | 0 | 3 |
| 7 | 4s | 8c | 2 | 3 |
| 8 | 4s | 9s | 3 | 4 |
| 9 | 1c | 6c | 0 | 2 |
| 10 | 4c | 3c | 1 | 3 |
| 11 | 2c | 3c | 1 | 1 |
| 12 | 0s | 3s | 0 | 3 |
| Physician assistants | | | | |
| 1 | 6c | 2s | 2 | 3 |
| 2 | 2c | 4s | 2 | 2 |
| 3 | 1s | 2c | 3 | 3 |
| 4 | 0c | 1c | 2 | 2 |
| 5 | 0c | 4s | 1 | 1 |
| 6 | 1c | 3c | 0 | 1 |
| 7 | 0c | 3c | 0 | 1 |
| 8 | 2c | 4c | 1 | 3 |
| Total | 12 | 23 | 11 | 16 |
| Nurse anesthetists | | | | |
| 1 | 5s | 6s | 2 | 3 |
| 2 | 3s | 8s | 2 | 1 |
| 3 | 4s | 3c | 3 | 4 |
| 4 | 1c | 3s | 2 | 0 |
| 5 | 5s | 1c | 1 | 1 |
| 6 | 2s | 2c | 1 | 3 |
| 7 | 2s | 3s | 2 | 3 |
| Total | 22 | 26 | 13 | 15 |

s = substitute; c = complement.

### Table 3. Frequencies of Resistance by Key Informants

| Resistance examples | |
| --- | --- |
| Nurse practitioners | |
| 1 | 4s |
| 2 | 5s |
| 3 | 4s |
| 4 | 3s |
| 5 | 4s |
| 6 | 3c |
| Total | 23 |
| Physician assistants | |
| 1 | 2c |
| 2 | 1c |
| 3 | 3c |
| 4 | 2c |
| 5 | 4c |
| 6 | 3c |
| Total | 15 |
| Nurse anesthetists | |
| 1 | 5s |
| 2 | 4s |
| 3 | 3c |
| 4 | 5s |
| 5 | 6s |
| Total | 23 |

## Provider's Views: Extent of 'Substitutability'

Each of the providers varied in the extent to which they considered themselves a substitute provider. CRNAs considered themselves as substitute providers more often than a complement, while NPs were somewhat mixed (refer to table 2). PAs viewed themselves as a complement more often than a substitute. Not surprisingly, those who considered themselves a 'complementary' provider reported less resistance compared to those who considered themselves a substitute. Meanwhile, male 'complementary' providers had fewer examples of devalued labour compared to females. This suggests that gender may play more of a role in resistance to mid-level providers than initially thought.

## AREAS OF LEAST RESISTANCE

There were several areas where physicians did not appear to put up as much resistance perhaps because they viewed these as less desirable areas to practice in. Three key areas of 'least resistance' emerged from the interviews: (1) devalued tasks; (2) less desirable patient groups; (3) and devalued geographical locations. Indeed, conflicts over boundaries can result in the subordination of one profession by another where unwanted tasks are discarded (Halpern 1992; Hugman 1991).

## Devalued Tasks

Most providers performed at least one task that they felt was devalued that physicians did not want to perform such as admissions, health promotion and counselling. For example, "if physicians can avoid doing an admission, certainly they'd rather I did it because it's time consuming" (Male NP #1).

To a certain extent the work in the pre-admission clinic is something that the physician's don't have time to do. They might see it as turfing. (Male NP #2)

Health promotion activities often fell more to NPs and PAs, which is in part, why the role was created.

Although NPs do diagnose and treat minor illnesses and injuries the majority of their time at work is spent on the health promotion, the disease prevention, the rehabilitative stuff. (Female NP #5)

I probably do more of the immunizations and well-child, well-baby exams. The other service that I provide here that the doctors don't normally do is foot care to patients, especially diabetics and patients with mobility problems. (Male NP #2)

Some reported that women's exams or more trivial tasks were given to them. For example, a male PA (#2) said he did "all the suturing. Generally, anything that needs sewing becomes mine. They tend not to like to do sewing which is kind of ironic. I would say half the doctors I work with leave all that for me." Others claimed that physicians would work on the patients that would make the most money:

I could do the entire work-up and physical assessment and take the history because they'd [physicians] rather not do that, while they see all the lower acuity patients because that would make more money. (Female NP #3)

Anesthesia, where CRNAs often handled the complex cases, was a sharp contrast compared to PAs and NPs who often performed more of the trivial and less costly tasks. For example:

In most nurse anesthetist practices the physicians don't actually do the 'hands-on' anesthesia. If they do it they usually do the lighter type of cases like in radiation and cat scans because they can cover those cases independently. They'll have the nurses do the bigger, more complex cases. (Female CRNA #4)

At our hospital the anesthesiologists will stop by the room at induction and watch the nurse anesthetist put the patient to sleep and put in the tube and then osculate the patient's chest. Then they walk out of the room. (Female CRNA #6)

Another CRNA similarly claimed: "Anesthesiologists are perfectly content to sit in the office and drink their coffee while we're doing the work. Most of the hand-on beating the bag work is done by CRNAs" (Female CRNA #5). Others reported:

There are places where anesthesiologists are more than happy to sit in a room and just provide the anesthetic and let the attendings do the central venous lines, arterial lines and the fiber optic intubations and look at the fact that they're compensated well as more than enough. They're not interested in the additional responsibility or liability. (Male CRNA #4)

This may be a result of the way anesthesiologists and CRNAs are reimbursed. Given that anesthesiologists are allowed to supervise up to four CRNAs at a time and can bill for their services (AANA 2006), they may be inclined to let them do most of the work.

Each of the provider groups performed devalued labour to some extent. Female NPs reported the highest number of devalued examples while male NPs had the least (refer to table 2). The rest of the providers were approximately the same with females reporting slightly more devalued examples than males. This suggests that gender may play an important role in the tasks performed. It seems that PAs and NPs were 'ditched the dirty work' while CRNAs seemed to perform almost all the tasks because of the way anesthesiologists are reimbursed. In sum, NPs and PAs performed different, albeit devalued tasks while CRNAs performed many of the same tasks as anesthesiologists.

## Less Desirable Patient Groups and Specialty Areas

Another key theme that emerged was that mid-level providers tend to practice more often in less desirable practice areas and/or patient groups. For example, a much greater proportion of NPs and PAs worked in general practice compared to physicians (refer to table 4). Physician's interest in family medicine has declined because the specialty areas offer more pay and prestige (White and Herlihy 2003).

### Table 4. Proportion of Physicians and Mid-level Providers in Family Practice

| Specialty Area | |
| --- | --- |
| General/Family practitioner | 12.8% |
| Nurse Practitioner | 41.0% |
| Physician Assistant | 28.4% |

Sources: AAPA 2005; ACNP 2004; Bureau of Labor Statistics 2006).

There is a similar situation for CRNAs who increasingly perform obstetric anesthesia. CRNAs "are the main providers of obstetrical anesthesia in the US" (Nadolny 2000:1). For example, "In the hospital where I was, the nurse anesthetists did all the OB, the anesthesiologists did all of the OR" (Female CRNA #1). This may be a result of the amount of time and care involved or perhaps greater pay. Some providers reported:

We weren't allowed to go into the OR. The anesthesiologists had the contract for the operating room and we worked directly as employees of the hospital in OB. Now, they ran a pre-anesthesia clinic and we did not participate in that at all. I would go see patients in the anesthesia office if they needed a pre-anesthesia assessment. They would just call me and let me know then I would go to their office at their next appointment and see them. But there are definite practice patterns. Some places the nurse anesthetists don't take call at all. Most of the time the nurse anesthetists do rotate through call. But there are practices where the anesthesiologists are the only ones placing epidurals and spinals, doing regional anesthesia techniques even though the nurse anesthetists have been trained in that and are competent in it. It's just the way their practice is.

A CRNA working in OB has to be part social worker, part psychologist and have the knowledge about anesthesia and obstetrics to adequately care for these patients (Farella 2000). The findings in this research similarly suggest:

> Anesthesiologists do not want to deal with an awake patient, which is undesirable because it requires reassuring the patient and making them feel comfortable....To meet the needs of one patient and one family member an obstetrician and a couple of nurses all at the same time, which is often times what you have to do in obstetric anesthesia. Those are probably the main reasons why they don't like OB. (Female CRNA #4)

Some NPs and PAs commented on how 'difficult' patients and certain populations tended to be less desirable among physicians. For example, "If it's a whiner or complainer type patient you may slough them off to me" (Female NP #2). Other NPs had similar examples:

> We have a very difficult population that we work with. They take more time... It's a poor part of the town. Much more complex cases than you would see in a middle-class practice. We have dysfunctional families. Language problems; A lot of socio-economic problems in the area. It's much more complex and some of the physical problems can be pretty complex too. In fact we had one new physician practicing over on the other side of town and he called up one day and asked us if we would take this patient because he was too complex for his practice. He was looking for the fast and dirty way to do it. (Female NP #6)

Another NP said she worked "in very under-served areas and people usually don't want to go that route...these are current druggies, HIV positive, hepatitis C positive patients" (Female NP #3). Others had similar experiences: "The population that I serve, they're transient people" (Female NP #1).

> We have more complex issues with this elderly population. Physicians can't possibly see all those people, so we sort of augment the health care team by being able to spend a little bit more time with people doing the health teaching and so on. (Female NP #1)

Interestingly, it seemed to be mostly female NPs and some female PAs who reported working with these particular groups. This may help to explain why females reported more devalued tasks compared to males (refer to table 2).

## Less Desirable Geographical Areas

Each of the providers, especially NPs and CRNAs reported how rural areas seemed less desirable to physicians. There is a greater proportion of NPs compared to primary care physicians (refer to table 5). At the same time, there is almost twice as many CRNAs in rural areas (18.6%) compared to CRNAs (8.4%). This sheds light on why a greater proportion of

NPs and CRNAs considered themselves a substitute provider rather than a complement. Indeed, these providers often fill gaps in areas with physician shortages. Several mid-level providers gave examples of how rural areas were less desirable:

> Anesthesiologists don't want to work in undesirable areas. They are not well reimbursed. (Female CRNA #2).

> I 100% know that this opportunity came about because it was rural. The docs didn't want to travel out here, so that's why it became an opportunity for a nurse practitioner. (Female NP #2)

### Table 5. Practice Location of Physicians and Mid-level Providers

|                          | Rural  | Urban  |
|--------------------------|--------|--------|
| Primary care physicians  | 22%    | 78%    |
| Nurse Practitioner       | 25%    | 75%    |
| Physician Assistant      | 16.6%  | 83.4%  |
| Anesthesiologist         | 8.4%   | 91.6%  |
| Nurse Anesthetist        | 18.6%  | 81.4%  |

Sources: AAPA 2005; Fallacaro and Ruiz-Law 2004; NSSRN 2000).

Another CRNA commented that anesthesiologists tend not to work in low paying communities.

> You'll find a lot of nurse anesthetists in under-served communities because anesthesiologists gravitate to communities that have more money...There's very few anesthesiologists in rural communities. I think that's true country wide. There are few anesthesiologists in the urban-poor communities. (Male CRNA #3)

The interviews also suggested that physicians do not put up as much resistance when mid-level providers are substituting in areas that are not as desirable; however, as soon as they are on the turf that is worth protecting they tend to resist. For example:

> You can't get away from the fact that in certain areas, you really are substituting in the more remote areas. It's hard enough getting doctors there. (Female NP #1)

> The medical association has always been quite opposed to nurse practitioners to doing anything other than under the direction of a physician, We know that we have nurse practitioners in rural areas who are quite capable of doing certain things when there's no docs around, but as soon as you get within a 100 miles of a doctor there's the sense that they're not capable of doing things. (NP key informant #3)

In sum, there were several areas where physicians did not appear to put up as much resistance perhaps because they viewed these as less desirable areas to practice in. These included devalued tasks, less desirable patient groups, and devalued geographical locations.

# CONCLUSION

This chapter examined the extent to which mid-level providers experienced resistance from physicians. Although in the past medicine maintained a monopoly, competitors have increasingly encroached on their territory, placing pressure on existing professional boundaries. The results suggest that the amount of medical resistance varied by type of provider and their extent of 'substitutability.' Jurisdictional disputes seemed most evident around the areas that were most valued to physicians, while there was less resistance around the fringes (i.e., less desirable areas). This may be a result of physicians wanting to maintain their autonomy and dominance.

Key tensions arose around financial concerns and maintaining medical dominance, while other physicians were resistant because they lacked knowledge of the role. This is consistent with research showing that physician's are often reluctant to support mid-level providers because they are concerned about jurisdiction and/or are unfamiliar with the role (Macay 2003; Martin and Hutchinson 1999).

The mid-level providers in this study experienced resistance from both the political level and in day-to-day practice. The extent of resistance encountered in this study varied by gender and type of provider. Many of the providers discussed how medical associations often put up road blocks to prevent them from gaining more independence. It was interesting to note that PAs experienced less resistance than NPs and CRNAs, which may stem from their similar backgrounds to physicians. This is consistent with past findings indicating that physician's attitudes towards PAs are more favorable than towards other providers which may be due to their closer ties with medicine (Johnson and Freeborn 1986).

Political road-blocks were also felt on a more personal level in day-to-day practice. Female NPs reported more resistance than others, while male NPs and PAs experienced the least. Female NPs also reported more examples of devalued work while others reported it less often. This may have been a result of the devaluation of women's work, which is especially salient with nurse practitioners. Interestingly, females experienced resistance on more of a personal level while males described it more at the political level.

Each type of provider varied in the extent to which they considered themselves a substitute provider. CRNAs saw themselves as substitute providers more often than a complement, while NPs were somewhat mixed. Meanwhile, PAs viewed themselves as a complement more often than a substitute. Those who considered themselves a 'complementary' provider reported less resistance compared to those who considered themselves a substitute—suggesting that physicians may resist more when their territory is being threatened.

There were three key areas where physicians did not appear to put up as much resistance towards mid-level providers: devalued tasks, less desirable patient groups and devalued geographical locations. Most of the providers routinely performed tasks that were devalued by physicians such as admissions, health promotion and sewing. Mid-level providers experienced less resistance in rural and under-served areas and less desirable specialty areas and patient groups. This is consistent with previous research reporting that non-physician providers have "historically thrived in settings where physicians were unavailable—places where they were unable or unwilling to go" (Flanagan 1998: 2).

The results suggest that there may have been an active discarding of unwanted tasks, or 'ditching the dirty work' to the mid-levels (Hugman 1991; Nancarrow and Borhickos 2005). This is consistent with Hughes (1958) who found that those with the greatest professional standing retained the most desirable work, delegating less pleasant work to others. This was the case not only between physicians and mid-levels but by gender as well, where women reported more resistance. This may have been a result of traditional doctor-nurse relations and the devaluation of women's work. This is consistent with Cohen et al. (1998) who found that most NPs expressed concerns of being 'invisible' providers and felt that their services were not recognized as being major contributing factors to the overall services that were provided.

The encroachment of mid-level providers onto physician's territory has heightened battles over professional jurisdiction. There remains a lack of clarity over certain areas of professional jurisdiction because it appears to vary by place and specialty area. The resistance encountered by mid-level providers can largely be attributed to physicians trying to protect their turf. Interestingly, mid-level providers encountered less resistance in the areas that were not deemed worthy of protecting. This 'ditching of the dirty work' or less desirable skills may be a way of ensuring that they maintain dominance.

This study addressed several gaps in the health professions literature by focusing on mid-level provider's experience while highlighting gender differences and insight from key informants. There has been relatively little examination of mid-level provider's experience of medical resistance while drawing on several different occupations and exploring gender differences. Most research focuses on the cost-effectiveness of such providers and physicians' and clients' views of them, yet little is known about the experiences of mid-level providers and how professional dynamics are shaped by their presence. Much of the literature has focused on the impact of mid-level providers on physicians. Given the increased reliance on mid-level providers in an effort to save money and fill gaps in physician shortages, it is important to examine their experiences. Understanding the extent of medical resistance that such providers may experience is valuable because it could help with job satisfaction, inter-professional relations and recruitment/retention strategies and patient care (Amost and Lasinger 2002; Neale 1999).

In conclusion, the extent of resistance experienced by mid-level providers varied by the extent of the extent of 'substitutability' (independence) of the provider and also by gender. The greatest amount of resistance was experienced in areas where physicians felt the most threatened. The findings also suggest that gender may play an important role in mid-level provider's experience of medical resistance. Future research should be directed to several areas. First, researchers should compare physician's views with mid-level providers because discrepancies appear to exist. Second, more examination is needed of why females experienced resistance at a more personal level, while males at more of a political level. Finally, further studies should explore why women reported more resistance and more examples of devalued tasks.

## ACKNOWLEDGEMENTS

Funding for this reserach was provided through a doctoral fellowship from the Canadian Institutes of Health Research.

# REFERENCES

Abbott, A. (1988). *The System of Professions.* Chicago: University of Chicago Press.

American Academy of Family Practitioners (AAFP). (2006). *Non-Physician Providers.* AAFP: Policy and Advocacy.

American Academy of Nurse Practitioners. (2006). *Nurse practitioners as an advanced practice nurse: role position statement.* Washington: AANP.

American Academy of Physician Assistants. (2006). *AAPA Physician Assistant Census Report.* AAPA.

American Association of Nurse Anesthetists (2003). *Nurse Anesthetists At A Glance.* www.aana.com/crna/ataglance.asp

American Association of Nurse Anesthetists. (2006). *Medicare Reimbursement.* www.aana.com/resources/practice documents

American College of Nurse Practitioners. (2004). *US Nurse Practitioner Workforce.* ACNP Member Survey.

Amost, J. and Laschinger, H. (2002). Workplace empowerment, collaborative work relationships, and job strain in nurse practitioners. *Journal of the American Academy of Nurse Practitioners,* 14 (9), 408-419.

Aquilino, M., Damiano, P., Willard, J., Mamany E., and Levey, B. (1999). Primary care physician perceptions of the nurse practitioner in the 1990s. *Archives of Family Medicine,* 8, 224-227.

Armstrong, P. and Armstrong, H. (2003). *Wasting Away: The Undermining of Canadian Health Care.* Toronto: Oxford University Press.

Auerbach, D. (2000). Nurse practitioners and primary care physicians: complements, substitutes and the impact of managed care. *Harvard Health Policy Review,* 1(1), 1-4.

Bankert, M. (1989). *Watchful Care.* New York: Continuum.

Birenbaum, R. (1994). Nurse practitioners and physicians: competition or collaboration? *Canadian Medical Association Journal,* 151(1), 76-78.

Bureau of Health Professions. (2000). *Health Resources and Service Administration State Health Workforce Profiles.* Maryland: U.S. Department of Health and Human Services.

Bureau of Labor Statistics. (2006). Physicians and surgeons. *Occupational Outlook Handbook.* US Department of Labor.

Butter, I., Carpenter, E., Kay, B., and Simmons, R. (1987). Gender hierarchies in the health labor force. *International Journal of Health Services,* 17(1), 133-149.

Calpin-Davies P. and Akehurst, R. (1999). Doctor-nurse substitution: The workforce equation. *Journal of Nursing Management,* 7(2), 71-9.

Cesa, F. and Larente, S. (2004). Workforce shortages: A question of supply and demand. *Health Policy Research Bulletin,* 8, 12-16.

Cchen, S., Mason, D. and Arsenie, L. (1998). Focus groups reveal perils and promises of managed care for nurse practitioners. *Nurse Practitioner,* 23(6), 48-77.

Conrad, H. (1992). Medicalization and Social Control. *Annual Review of Sociology.*

Cooper, R. (2001). Health care workforce for the twenty-first century: The impact of non-physician clinicians. *Annual Review of Medicine,* 52, 51-61.

Cooper, R., Henderson, T. and Dietrich, C. (1998a). Roles of nonphysician clinicians as autonomous providers of patient care. *Journal of the American Medical Association,* 280(9), 795-802.

Cooper, R., Laud, P. and Dietrich, C. (1998b). Current and projected workforce of nonphysician Clinicians. *Journal of the American Medical Association,* 280(9), 78-79.

Deuben, C. (1998). The impact of managed care on labor substitution in the health care workforce. *Michigan Academian,* 30(1), 69-83.

Drus, B., Marcus, S., Olfson, M., Tanielian T., and Pincus, H. (2003). Trends in care by nonphysician clinicians in the United States. *New England Journal of Medicine,* 348(2), 130-137.

Eaton, G. and Webb, B. (1979). Boundary encroachment: pharmacists in the clinical setting. *Sociology of Health and Illness,* 1(1), 69-89.

Fallacaro, M. and Ruiz-Law, T. (2004). Distribution of US anesthesia providers and services. *AANA Journal,* 72(1), 9-14.

Farella, C. (2000). Nurse anesthetists put an end to OB pain. *Nursing Spectrum,* April 17.

Flanagan, L. (1998). Nurse practitioners: growing competition for family physicians? *American Academy of Family Physicians,* October.

Freidson, E. (1970). *Profession of Medicine: A Study of the Sociology of Applied Knowledge.* New York: Harper and Row.

Friedson, E. (1988). *Profession of Medicine.* Chicago: University of Chicago Press.

Germov, J. (1998). Challenges to medical dominance. In Germov. Second Opinion: An *Introduction to Health Sociology.* Melbourne: Oxford University Press.

Green, J. and Thorogood, N. (2004). *Qualitative Methods for Health Research,* London, Sage.

Grumbach, K. and Coffman, J. (1998). Physicians and nonphysician clinicians. *Journal of the American Medical Association,* 280, 825-826.

Grumbach, K, Hart, L., Mertz, E., Coffman, J. and Palazzo, L. (2003). Who is caring for the underserved? *Annals of Family Medicine,* 1, 97-104.

Grzybicki D, Sullivan, P., Oppy, J., Bethke, J. and Raab, S. (2002). The economic benefit for family/general medicine practices employing physician assistants. *American Journal of Managed Care,* 8(7), 613-620.

Hafferty, F. and D. Light. (1995). Professional dynamics and the changing nature of medical work. *Journal of Health and Social Behavior.* (extra issue): 132-153.

Halpern, S. (1992). Dynamics of professional control: Internal coalitions and cross-professional boundaries. *American Journal of Sociology,* 97(4), 994-1021.

Hughes, E. (1958). *Men and their work.* Toronto: Free Press of Glencoe.

Hugman, R. (1991). *Power in Caring Professions.* London: Macmillan.

Johnson, R. and Freeborn, D. (1986). Comparing HMO physicians' attitudes towards NPs and PAs. *Nurse Practitioner,* 39-49.

Krapohl, G. and Larson, E. (1996). The impact of unlicensed assistive personnel on nursing care delivery. *Nursing Economics,* 14(2), 99-110.

Laurant, M. Reeves, D., Hermens, R., Braspenning, J., Grol, R. and Sibbald, B. (2006). *Substitution of doctors by nurses in primary care.* Wiley: The Cochrane Collaboration.

MacDonald, J., and Katz, A. (2002). Physicians' perceptions of nurse practitioners. *Canadian Nurse,* 7(98), 28-31.

Mackay, B. (2003). General practitioners' perceptions of the nurse practitioners role. *New Zealand Medical Journal*, 115(1170), U365.

Martin, P. and Hutchinson, H. (1999). Nurse practitioners and the problem of discounting. *Journal of Advanced Nursing*, 29(10), 9-17.

Mittman, D., Cawley, J. and Fern, W. (2002). Physician assistants in the United States. *British Medical Journal* 325, 485-457.

Mundinger, M. (1994). Advanced-practice nursing--good medicine for physicians? *New England Journal of Medicine*, 330(3), 211-4.

Nadolny, M. (2000). National nurse anesthetists week: The profession of preventing pain. *CRNA*, 16(3): 1-2.

Nancarrow, S. and Borthwick, A. (2005). Dynamic professional boundaries in the healthcare workforce. *Sociology of Health and Illness, 897*-919.

National Sample Survey of Registered Nurses. (2000). *Appendix B: Survey Methodology*. Maryland: Bureau of Health Professions.

Neale, J. (1999). Nurse Practitioners and physicians: A collaborative practice. *Clinical Nurse Specialist*, 13(5): 252-258.

Oxford Dictionary. (2006). Online: http://www.oed.com/

Petersdorf, R. (1993). Primary care: medical students' unpopular choice. *American Journal of Public Health*, 83, 328-330.

Richards, L. (1999). *Using NVIVO in Qualitative Research*. Sage: London.

Torgersen, K. and Chamings, P. (1994). Examining collaborative relationships between anesthesiologists and certified registered nurse anesthetists in nurse anesthesia educational programs. *Journal of the American Association of Nurse Anesthetists*, 62(2), 139-148.

Turner, B. (1995). *Medical Power and Social Knowledge*. New York: Sage.

White, L. and N. Herlihy. (2003). Family practice and internal medicine. In Ballweg, Stolberg and Sullivan (Eds). *Physician Assistant*. Philadelphia: Saunders.

In: Industrial Psychology Research Trends
Editor: Ina M. Pearle, pp. 47-72

ISBN: 978-1-60021-825-5
© 2007 Nova Science Publishers, Inc.

**Chapter 3**

# MENTAL HEALTH IN THE WORKPLACE (A CASE STUDY AMONG PROFESSIONALS IN THE FINANCIAL SERVICES SECTOR)

## *Xiao Lu Wang[1], Hector W.H. Tsang[*2] and Kan Shi[3]*

[1] Institute of Psychology, Chinese Academy of Sciences
[2] Department of Rehabilitation Sciences,
The Hong Kong Polytechnic University
[3] Management School, Chinese Academy of Sciences

## ABSTRACT

This chapter reviews extant literature on mental health in the workplace. We give particular attention to different models of work stress and explain its relationship with job burnout and depression which are two common mental health problems at work. Although the tie between stress and mental health is well known, there is a dearth of research on exploring its relationship in specific occupations. In the second part of this book chapter, we present a case study on identifying the work stressors of professionals working in the financial services section in Hong Kong. Finally, suggestions are made as to research that needs to be conducted in the future with a view to raising the awareness of employers and employees on this issue and at the same time unveiling the possible etiologies, promoting good mental health practices, and maintaining a healthy working environment.

* Correspondence concerning this chapter should be addressed to Hector W.H. Tsang at: Department of Rehabilitation Sciences; The Hong Kong Polytechnic University; Hunghom, Kowloon, Hong Kong; Tel: 852 – 27666750; Fax: 852 – 23308656 ; Email: rshtsang@polyu.edu.hk

## BACKGROUND

Mental health is as important as physical health contributing to the overall well-being of individuals. It is an indispensable constituent of *Health* defined by the World Health Organization (WHO). Unfortunately, mental health and mental disorders have been largely neglected by the public. As a result, the world is suffering from an rapidly increasing burden of mental disorders, and a widening "treatment gap". To date, some 450 million people suffer from mental or behavioral disorders, accounting for 12% of the global burden of disease (WHO, 2001). However, only a minority of them receives essential treatment. Mental health budgets of many countries constitute less than 1% of their total health expenditures (WHO, 2001). Mental and behavioral disorders represent five of the 10 leading causes of disability worldwide which include major depression, schizophrenia, bipolar disorder, alcohol use, and obsessive-compulsive disorders. Because of the extent and pervasiveness of mental health problems, mental health has been officially recognized as a top priority by the WHO (WHO and ILO, 2000).

Work occupies at least one third of a person's time in his/her life. People's well-being in the workplace is the linchpin to their well-being and happiness. Contrarily, work setting could be a huge hidden trouble threatening people's well-being if it is dysfunctional. Along with the trend of globalization and rationalization of economy, organizations have been forced to upgrade their efficiency to adapt to this fast changing, unpredictable, and highly competitive environment. Workers bear heavier stress than ever before not only because of the high demands of work but also from the neglect of human needs in this economy-oriented world (Desjarlais et al, 1995; WHO and ILO, 2000). This, in turn, takes toll of employee's physical, psychological and behavioral health. Psychosocial stress has been proved to be harmful physiologically which may increase risk of high blood pressure, high cholesterol level, cardiovascular diseases, and gastrointestinal discomforts (Matteson and Ivancevich, 1979; Pollard, 2001). It has long been admitted as an important etiological factor of mental disorders according to the stress-diathesis model of psychopathology (Barlow and Durand, 1995). Work stress has a significant impact on workers' mental health and accounts for 41% of the variation in the general health (Iacovides et al., 2003). It is no doubt that workers are exposed to high risk of mental health problems. It is therefore timely to direct our attention towards preventing mental disturbances resulting from stress in the workplace, which will be the key to mitigating the global burden resulting from mental and behavioral disorders.

Although our knowledge of mental health issues has significantly increased over the past few decades, employers and enterprises lag behind in their awareness, understanding and acceptance of the pervasiveness, treatment and impact of mental health problems on organizational life. The problem and impairment of mental health in the workplace on the well being and productivity of employees has long been underestimated (WHO and ILO, 2000). Workers with mental health problems could cause a large amount of work disability which refers to interference of their ability to perform their work role. A classic example is "lost productivity" resulting from being unable to attend work which is referred to be *absenteeism*, usually calculated by *loss days*. On the other hand, lost productivity, calculated in *cutback days*, which arises from attending work while unwell, is known as *presenteeism* (Sanderson and Andrews, 2006). It is estimated that 20% of the adult working population in European Union countries has some type of mental health problems at any given time

[STAKES, 1999). Some 15 to 30% of workers in United Kingdom experience mental health problems during their working lives (UKDH, 1993). More than 40 million people in USA have mental health problems and 4 to 5 million adults of this population are considered seriously mentally ill (NIDRR, 1993). Mental illness is the third leading cause of disability to organizations which accounts for 7% costs of occupational and work-related diseases (ILO, 1999). The costs could be due to diminished productivity, insurance claim, and employee turnover which drive the figure up to 4 billion dollars each year (MHF, 2000). Given the above, the International Labour Organisation (ILO) has started to admit and claim that employee's mental health problems and their impact on an enterprise's productivity are critical human resource issues (WHO and ILO, 2000). The benefits to both individuals and the organization resulting from the promotion of good mental health at work include increased presence, well-being and productivity of workers.

## JOB BURNOUT AND DEPRESSION

### Job Burnout

Job burnout featured by exhaustion, cynicism, and reduced professional efficacy, is first recognized by practitioners and social commentators as a social problem of the dysfunctional relationships between people and their work in care-giving and human serving occupations (Maslach, Schaufeli, and Leiter, 2001). It is conceptualized as a psychological syndrome which involves a prolonged response to chronic emotional and interpersonal stressors on the job (Freudenberger, 1975; Maslash, 1976). Through years of efforts on empirical studies, job burnout has been endowed with richer meaning to be generalized to similar problems in all kinds of occupation. Along with this trend, its original three dimensions (i.e., emotional exhaustion, depersonalization and decreased personal accomplishment) have evolved into exhaustion, cynicism, and reduced professional efficacy. Exhaustion represents the basic and central quality of burnout which is the most obviously manifested aspect of this complex syndrome. Originally, it refers only to the emotional domain as the negative result of human-oriented jobs requiring workers to involve their emotion intentionally to facilitate work. But now it refers to feelings of being overextended and depleted of not only one's emotional but also physical resources. Depersonalization is proposed as a dysfunctional coping strategy towards this emotion-demanding stressor. It refers to the negative, callous and dehumanized ways workers use to keep themselves emotionally distant from their service recipients so as to protect themselves from intense emotional arousal. The newer concept of cynicism is an analogue of depersonalization which represents a negative, callous, or excessively detached response to various aspects of the job rather than only recipients. The third dimension is reduced professional efficacy which is the same as the original one referring to feeling of incompetence and a lack of achievement and productivity at work (Maslach, Schaufeli, and Leiter, 2001).

Maslach Burnout Inventory (MBI; Maslach and Jackon, 1986) has been the most utilized research instrument to measure burnout. Along with the modification of framework of job burnout, the instrument has developed versions specific to the human services sector (the MBI-Human Services Survey), and educational settings (the MBI-Educator Survey). A generic version is also available for applications to any occupations (the MBI-General Survey).

Job burnout can lead to a range of negative outcomes pertaining to organizations and workers. To organizations, burnout has been associated with various forms of job withdrawal, absenteeism, intention to leave the job, and actual turnover. For people who stay on the job, burnout leads to lower productivity and effectiveness at work. Moreover, organizational atmosphere could also be eroded by job burnout. It can be contagious and perpetuate itself through informal interactions on the job. Workers could be negatively influenced by their burned out colleagues through gloomy morale, personal conflict, and disrupting job tasks (Maslach, Schaufeli, and Leiter, 2001). To workers, job burnout is related to job dissatisfaction and lack of commitment to the job or the organization. There is also evidence that burnout has a negative "spillover" effect on people's home life (Burke and Greenglass, 2001). The status of being burned out is detrimental to health. It may cause various forms of substance abuse. The exhaustion component of burnout is found to be associated with physiological problems such as high blood pressure, high cholesterol level, and gastrointestinal problems. Similarly, it may cause mental problems such as job-related neurasthenia, depression, and anxiety (Maslach, Schaufeli, and Leiter, 2001).

"Burnout" is used and studied so frequently and tensely nowadays in work-related stress research that it has lost much of its original meaning and been generalized to describe everything from fatigue to depression. Job burnout is viewed as a counterpart of depression in work-related area by I/O psychologists and Organizational Behavior researchers. It has even become an alternative word for depression when it comes to work, but with a less serious significance (Liu and Van-Liew, 2003).

## Depression-Relevant Mental Problems in the Workplace

Depression is characterized by sadness, loss of interest in activities, and decreased energy which is the most prevalent mental disorder in the working population. It is estimated to be the most costly mental disorder to organizations (Sanderson and Andrews, 2006; WHO, 2001; Lerner et al., 2004). Prevalence rate of depression in the working population ranges from 2.2 to 4.8 % (Sanderson and Andrews, 2006). The cost of depression is at least $12.4 billion annually in medical care and $44 billion annually in lost productive work time (Lerner et al., 2004). The National Comorbidity Survey (Jenkins et al., 1997) reported even higher rates of depression among clerical or sales workers and laborers but lower rates among professionals and crafts people.

Two main depression relevant disorders in the workplace are adjustment disorder with depressed mood and major depressive disorder (DSM-IV; American Psychiatric Association, 1994). Adjustment disorder with depressed mood is an adjustment disorder to specific and identifiable psychosocial stressors (Liu and Van Liew, 2003). The depressed mood of the sufferers is transient. The nature of the disorder assumes that the disturbance will remit after the stressor ceases or when individual adaptations are made. The stressor, single or multiple, periodic or continuous, could accompany specific developmental and life events, such as getting married, becoming a parent, or changing to a new job. Such life events often occur in the workplace, such as underemployment, conflict with supervisor, heavy workload, and failing to attain work target. A stressor may affect only a particular individual, group or community, which depends on their perception of stress and vulnerabilities. Epidemiological evidence shows that 5 to 20 percent of the population suffers from the disorder (American Psychiatric Association, 1994). A full-blown depressive syndrome can develop from adjustment disorder with depressed mood, as long as the stressor is of enough intensity, duration and combined with the unique vulnerability of that person. Major depressive disorder (MDD) is the best known form of depression. It is commonly described as a 'nervous breakdown" or "chemical imbalance". In contrast to adjustment disorder, external stressors may or may not lead to an episode of a major depression. There is evidence that the initial episodes of a major depression are more likely to be triggered off by an external stressor. However, an obvious stressor is not necessarily required for its recurrences (Liu and Van Liew, 2003).

People diagnosed with depression may experience depressed mood, loss of interest, a considerable loss or gain of weight, difficulty falling or staying asleep, sleeping more than usual, behavior agitated or slowed down, fatigued, diminished energy, thoughts of worthlessness or extreme guilt (not about being ill), reduced ability to think, concentrate, or make decisions, frequent thoughts of death or suicide (with or without a specific plan), and attempt of suicide (American Psychiatric Association, 1994). The person's symptoms result in significant distress or difficulty in social functioning at home, work, or other important areas.

Depression, as a mood disorder, not only brings great loss to company on both productivity/cost and morale but also impairs the psychological well-being of workers and their quality of life (Barge-Schaapveld, 1999; Stewart et al., 2003). The negative influence of depression is more invisible and far-reaching due to its spiritually disabling nature. Previous research shows that productivity loss caused by depression increases with occupation's demand on decision-making, communication and frequent customer contact (Lerner et al., 2004).

## Differentiating Burnout and Depression

Depression and burnout are common mental health problems in the working populations today. They seem to be interrelated and there is a need therefore for their differential diagnosis (Ahola et al., 2005). A confusion of job burnout with depression causes both theoretical and practical problems.

Given the high prevalence of depression, confusing job burnout with depression in the workplace will underestimate the severity of depression and delay giving timely treatment and rehabilitation to depressed workers. This will cause loss to organizations and impair the overall well being of workers Based on previous research, we summarize in Table 1 a number of similarities and differences between burnout and depression in terms of symptoms, etiologies, sequence of occurrence, and occurring areas.

**Table 1. Similarities and Differences between Burnout and Depression**

| Comparison | | Burnout | Depression |
|---|---|---|---|
| Symptoms (Similarities-S; Differences-D) | S | Share many dysphoric symptoms, including fatigue, difficulty relaxing off work, and inability to concentrate (Bakker, Schaufeli, Demerouti et al., 2000; Brenninkmeyer, Van Yperen, & Buunk, 2001) Emotional exhaustion and depression share 12~38% of their variance over lowered energy and chronic fatigue symptoms; depersonalization and depression share 2~29% over social withdrawal and learned helplessness, and personal accomplishment and depression share 3-20% (Leiter & Durup, 1994; Schaufeli & Enzmann, 1998). Insomnia, a symptom of major depression, is also highly prevalent in individuals suffering from burnout (Bell, Davison, & Sefcik, 2002). Share several qualitative characteristics, especially in the more severe forms of burnout and in vulnerable individuals (Iacovides et al., 2003; Ahola, 2005). | |
| | D | A predominance of dysphoric symptoms such as mental or emotional exhaustion and fatigue An emphasis on mental and behavioral symptoms more than physical ones Work-related burnout symptoms Manifestation of symptoms in "normal" persons who did not suffer from psychopathology before Decreased effectiveness and work performance because of negative attitudes and behaviors. Most of these elements are represented in the diagnosis for job-related neurasthenia (WHO, 1992; Maslach & Schaufeli, 1993; Maslach, Schaufeli, & Leiter, 2001). | Differing from burnout in self-image of patients (Brenninkmeyer et al., 2001). In a confirmatory factor analytic study, the items of depression and burnout scales did not load on the same factor, but models with two second order factors resulted (Leiter & Durup, 1994; Bakker et al., 2000). |
| Etiologies (Similarities-S; Differences-D) | S | Probably share a common etiology (Glass and McKnight, 1996; a review of 18 studies) Shared variance due to their concurrent development (Shirom & Ezrachi, 2003) Individuals who are more depression-prone are more vulnerable to burnout (Maslach, Schaufeli, & Leiter, 2001). Both lead to presenteeism and absenteeism (Maslach, Schaufeli, & Leiter, 2001; Stewart et al.; 2003; ) | |
| | D | Work overload, lack of sense of controllability, dissatisfied reward, lack of sense of community affiliation, unfairness, and incongruent values (Maslach & Leiter; 1997). | Workload, job involvement, job controllability social support (Tennant, 2001; Ylipaavalniemi, 2005) |
| Sequence of occurrence | | Burnout could be a phase in the development of a depressive disorder (Leiter & Durup, 1994; Bakker et al., 2000; Iacovides et al., 2003) | |
| Occurring areas | | Specific to the work context (Bakker et al., 2000; Glass & McKnight, 1996) | whole life areas (Bakker et al, 2000) |

## Etiologies of Burnout and Depression

Stress-diathesis model of psychopathology (Barlow and Durand, 1995) suggests that stress is an important etiological factor of psychological disorders. It refers to a disruption of the equilibrium of the cognitive-emotional-environmental system by external factors, traditionally called stressors or stressful events (McGrath, 1976; Lazarus and Folkman, 1984; Demerouti, Bakker, Nachreiner and Schaufeli, 2001). The stressor poses a dynamic transaction between external demands and constraints, external supplies and supports, personal resources, and internal needs and values in which an individual strives to maintain balance (Cox and Mackay, 1981). If the individual fails to do so, the equilibrium of the cognitive-emotional-environmental system will be disrupted which will then generate stress and relevant psychological disorders (Daniels and Guppy, 1997). Diathesis describes our "vulnerability", a condition that makes one susceptible to developing a psychological disorder. Stressful events or stressors can precipitate psychological disorders when they impinge on underlying vulnerabilities that magnify the stressors' psychological impact (Blatt and Zuroff, 1992; Zuroff, Mongrain and Santor, 2004).

## STRESS AND NEGATIVE EXPERIENCES IN THE WORKPLACE

Based on job demands-resources models, job demands are viewed as physiological and psychological costs of workers (Hockey, 1993; Demerouti, Bakker, Nachreiner and Schaufeli, 2001) which may act as work stressors when they are high enough to cause psychological disorders (Karasek, 1979; Karasek and Theorell, 1990; van der Doef and Maes, 1999; de Lange et al., 2003). However, job resources including the material and the spiritual can be viewed as a counterbalancing force to the costs of job demand (Richter and Hacker, 1998) which in turn protects the health of workers from burnout or psychological disorders (Demerouti, Bakker, Nachreiner and Schaufeli, 2001). The effort-reward imbalance model regards work as a social contract between the employers and employees. Employees therefore have expectations of benefits and rewards resulting from work effort. When this contract is not reciprocated, effort-reward imbalance will result which makes the work environment act as a stressor and leads to adverse health outcomes of the employees (Siegrist, 1996, 2001; Tsutsumi and Kawakami, 2004). The two models mentioned above put emphasis on a transactional relationship between workers and job which corresponds to the transactional models of work stress. It underscored a dynamic transaction between external demands and constraints, external supplies and supports, personal resources, and internal needs and values that the individual strives to maintain a balance (Cox and Mackay, 1981).

Person-environment fit models well integrate the key points of aforementioned work stress models, and shed light on the importance of physical and psychological balance/fit between the person and his/her work to worker's well being (Edwards, 1991; Kristof, 1996; Judge and Cable, 1997; Kristof-Brown, 2000; Schneider, 2001; Cable and DeRue, 2002; Saks and Ashforth, 1997, 2002). Studies of person-environment (PE) fit have been prevalent in the management literature for almost 100 years (Jansen and Kristof-Brown, 2006) and this concept has become one of the most pervasive concepts in psychology (Schneider, 2001). It is particularly prominent in work stress research (Edwards and Cooper, 1990). This prominence is largely due to the conceptual advantages of the P-E fit approach over alternative approaches, most notably in which stress is viewed as a condition or event in a given situation (Cooper and Marshall, 1976; Hall and Mansfield, 1971; Matteson and Ivancevich, 1979) or as a psycho-physiological response of a focal person (Ivancevich and Matteson, 1980; Parker and DeCotiis, 1983). The P-E fit approach regards cognitive appraisal as the subjective comparison of person to environment and by distinguishing this comparison process from its outcomes (Edwards, 1996). No matter which level the fit is on (e.g., job level, vocational level, group level, and organizational level) or which mode the fit takes, all fits could be categorized into supplementary fit and complementary fit (Muchinsky and Monahan, 1987). Supplementary fit refers to the similarities between individual characteristics and organizational and vocational characteristics on values, goals, personality, etc. In contrast, complementary fit means individual and environment satisfy each other's needs or demands with resources or supplies the other side does not have. The resources on the organizational or vocational side could include money, reputation, etc, while on the worker's side they could be KSAs (i.e., knowledge, skills, and abilities), time, effort, etc (Kristof, 1996). Previous study shows that value incongruence and needs (at worker's side)-supplies (by work environment) unfit play unique and an equal roles in affecting work attitudes such as lowered organizational commitment, job dissatisfaction, and organizational unfairness which impair worker's psychological well-being. Alternatively, demands-abilities fit had a substantially weaker effect on attitudes. It did, however, show relatively equal effects on strain (e.g., job burnout) and performance as the other forms of fit (Tsutsumi and Kawakami, 2004; Cable and Edwards, 2004; Kristof-Brown, Zimmerman, and Johnson, 2005).

In the light of Kristof (1996)'s proposition, we summarize the above models and factors relevant to negative experiences and stress in the workplace in figure 1. As shown in the figure, there are four major fits (i.e., value congruence, job demands-abilities fit, needs-supplies fit, and effort-rewards fit) contributing to experiences in the workplace including work attitudes, stress and behaviors.

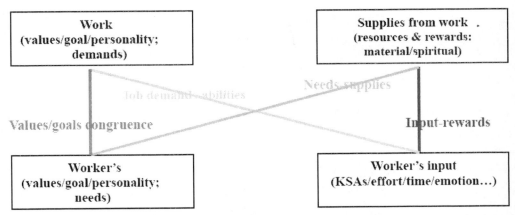

Note.  Values/goals/personality congruence usually result in organizational commitment, job engagement, and so on; job demands-abilities unfit mainly causes job burnout; needs-supplies unfit primarily leads to job dissatisfaction; input-rewards imbalance elicits sense of unfairness.

Figure 1. Person-Environment Fits in the Workplace.

# DIATHESES

Diatheses include biological and psychological vulnerabilities (Zubin and Spring, 1977; Barlow and Durand, 1995). In this chapter, we will focus on psychological vulnerabilities which include the cognitive and personality aspects. Previous studies emphasized the role of cognitive vulnerabilities as mediator or catalyst through which job stressors precipitate the onset of depression in the workplace (Lazarus, Delongis, Folkman and Gruen, 1985; Daniels and Guppy, 1997). Research efforts (Abramson, Alloy, and Hankin, 2002; Sadock et al., 2004) show that cognitive vulnerabilities include negative attributional style (Seligman, 1975; Abramson, Metalsky and Alloy, 1989), dysfunctional attitudes (Blatt, et al., 1983, 1992; Beck, 1983, 1987, 1996; Zuroff, Mongrain, and Santor, 2004), and ruminative response style (Nolen-Hoeksema, 1991). The hopelessness theory suggests that people are more likely to become depressed when a stressor is attributed to stable (i.e., persisting over time) and global (i.e., affecting multiple areas in life) causes; perceived as leading to other negative consequences in the future; viewed as implying something negative about the self (e.g., worthlessness); and uncontrollable and feeling hopelessness on relief from undesirable events. Dysfunctional attitudes theory states that depression-prone individuals possess negative self-beliefs. They have a negative view of themselves, seeing themselves as worthless, unlovable, and deficient. They have a negative view of their environment, seeing it as overwhelming, filled with obstacles and failure. Finally they have a negative view of their future, seeing it as hopeless and believing that no effort will change their lives. These three factors are considered to be the cognitive triad. This negative way of thinking guides one's perceptions, interpretations, and memory of personally relevant experiences resulting in a negative worldview and depression. A ruminative response style describes behaviors and thoughts that bias a person's attention on his/her depressive symptoms.

Other than cognitive vulnerabilities, personality is a significant precipitator of depression. Existing research shows that dependency/sociotropy and self-criticism/autonomy (Blatt et al., 1976, 1983, 1992; Zuroff, 2004; Beck, 1983, 1996), neuroticism (Coyne and Whiffen, 1995), locus of control (Kobasa, Maddi and Kahn, 1982; Spector, 1982, 1988, 1994; Daniels and Guppy, 1997), and Type A behavior pattern (Friedman and Rosenman, 1974; Bluen, Barling and Burns, 1990) are of particular importance. Dependency/Sociotropy consists of traits related to excessive interpersonal dependency and a strong need for affiliation and support from others. Self-criticism/autonomy includes traits related to excessive achievement expectations and a strong need for independence. Neuroticism refers to emotional instability, vulnerability to stress and a proneness to anxiety (Eysenck, 1968). Type A behavior pattern (Friedman and Rosenman, 1974) is characterized by a continuous, deeply ingrained struggle to overcome real and imagined obstacles imposed by events, people, and time. Type A behaviors represents an effort to diminish an underlying sense of insecurity or self-doubt. Unfortunately, this behavior tends to set a self-defeating cycle in motion. As to locus of control, it is a personality construct referring to an individual's perception of the locus of events as determined internally by his/her own behavior vs fate, luck, or external circumstances (Spector, 1982, 1988, 1994). External locus of control has been found to have a negative relationship with psychological disorders such as depression and anxiety (Beekman et al., 2000).

## Interface between Work and Non-Work Domains

Depression is a pervasive disorder which affects a wide range of life areas. Then next logical question is whether negative experiences in the workplace spillover to non-work domains which in turn affects the whole life. Interactions between work and non-work domains take either practical or spiritual ways. Work-family conflict model demonstrates the practical influences. Time spent in work or family domain, gender, demand on taking care of child, spouse, or old parents have been identified as factors contributing to work-family conflict (Ford, Heinen, Langkamer, 2007). Stress from the work domain is the strongest correlate with interference of work in family and family satisfaction. On the other hand, family stress and family conflict are the strongest family-domain correlates of job satisfaction although not as strong as those between job stress and family satisfaction (Ford, Heinen, Langkamer, 2007).

With regards to spiritual influences, it concerns the effects of negative work experiences on changes of attitudes toward characteristics or objects in non-work domains due to the key role of negative attitude triad in depression (Beck, 1983, 1987, 1996). Given that there is not any negative event in non-work areas which could explicitly be attributed, the attitude change could be brought about by negative work experiences followed by a series of implicit processes such as mood spillover effect (Edwards and Rothbard, 2000), falsely attribution of negative emotion caused by negative work experiences to non-work areas being bad (Schwarz & Clore, 1983, 2003), evaluative conditioning in which CS (conditioned stimulus, e.g., non-work areas) acquires affective qualities of US (unconditioned stimulus, e.g., work area) by mere spatio-temporal CS-US co-occurrences or adjacency rather than signal or expectancy learning (i.e., classical conditioning) (Baeyens, Hermans, & Eelen, 1993; Rozin et al., 1998; Walther, 2002; e Houwer, Baeyens, & Field, 2005), mood-congruent memories retrieving in which negative moods spillovered from negative work experiences elicit negative interpretations of events and retrieve unpleasant memories, thoughts and feelings (Rusting & DeHart, 2000).

# CASE STUDY IN THE HONG KONG SPECIAL ADMINISTRATIVE REGION OF CHINA; WORK STRESS OF PROFESSIONALS IN FINANCIAL SERVICES SECTORS

Along with the globalization of the world economy and economic rationalization, the working environment for those working in the financial services sector has borne higher risks and more uncertainties, more frequent organizational/job restructuring, more competitive atmosphere, and greater job demands (Tennant, 2001; Tsutsumi and Kawakami, 2004; Montgomery, Blodgett and Barnes, 1996). This in turn adds more work-related stress among professional people such as securities and commodities sales agents, and financial consultants (Siu, 1996; Montgomery, Blodgett and Barnes, 1996; Grosch and Murphy, 1998; BLS, 2003; NIOSH; 2004). Stress could cause a wide range of mental health problems (Coyne and Whiffen, 1995). Emerging evidence has shown that employees in the financial services industry are increasingly more susceptible to psychological disorders including depression (Grosch and Murphy, 1998; Cass, 2000; BLS, 2003). Hong Kong, as one of the international finance centers, plays a key role in the stability and development of world economy. Investigating the etiology and impairment of depression among workers in the financial services sector is essential to the prevention of impairment on their health and productivity, which will contribute to the continuing economic prosperity of Hong Kong.

A growing body of evidence shows that there is a link between mental illness among workers and work-related stress. Both of these are likely to be related to occupation and work environment. We put our focus on the financial services sector because pertaining occupations are assumed to be highly susceptible to depression and could be viewed as a representative sample. Occupations in the financial services sector bear some key characters which could predispose workers to be vulnerable to depression. These characters have been identified as "client-related" stressors which typically exist in "caring" professions such as teachers, doctors, nurses, etc. (Tennant, 2001). A plethora of research efforts have been put into these occupations to investigate the mechanism of onset of depression and its intervention. However, little is currently known about the stressors in occupations of the financial services industry such as securities and commodities sales agents, and financial consultants whose duties possess key "occupational vulnerabilities", especially given the greater emphasis on the individualized and client-oriented service culture nowadays (Tennant, 2001). For example, a financial services salesperson must stress intangible benefits that often are not readily discernable by consumers. Financial services salespersons are not able to provide free samples and cannot readily demonstrate their product/service. Because of the intangible nature of financial services, service quality is more difficult for consumers to judge. Given the above, financial services typically are perceived to have a high degree of risk (Murray and Schlacter, 1990).

Depressive symptoms are harmful to the work ability of employees when the occupation has high demands on frequent customer contact, decision-making and communication (Lerner et al., 2004). Behavioral manifestations of depression during the work include marked decrease in job performance, frequently missing deadlines, working more slowly than usual, making excuses for not completing work, frequently calling in sick, appearing listless, being unable to concentration, frequently looking distracted or "far away", showing decreased involvement in work, withdrawal from interaction with coworkers, low energy, exaggerated self-doubts, indecisiveness, repeating a job, feeling fatigue at work, and presenteeism (Lerner et al., 2004; Stewart et al., 2003; Lanier, 2003; Berndt, et al., 1998; Johnson and Indvik, 1997)

Employees in the financial services industry are becoming more susceptible to depression with a prevalence rate of 1.1 per 10,000 full-time workers (Grosch and Murphy, 1998; Cass, 2000; BLS, 2003). It was found that higher rates of co-morbid mental disorders exist among professionals, middle management and unskilled clerical workers (Dewa and Lin, 2000).

This study aimed at identifying stressors and etiological factors of depression among stockbrokers in the workplace. The results will act as the foundation for further study among psychological well-being and productivity of workers in the financial services sector in Hong Kong and the mainland China.

# METHOD

## Participants

Twenty semi-structured interviews were conducted to a cohort of workers in the financial services sector in Hong Kong. They were randomly recruited from a list of licensed brokers in Hong Kong Securities and Future Commission. Participants who had any of following conditions were excluded from the study: bereavement, pregnancy/postpartum, alcohol/drug dependence, life-threatening physical illness, family psychiatric history, and tenure as stockbroker < 1 years. In terms of their work experience, eight of them have 1-3 years of work experience, five of them have 4-9 years work experience, and seven of them have 10 years of work experience. Their educational level ranged from secondary five to master degree. Four interviewees were below tertiary, three were at tertiary level, and thirteen were bachelor and above. Regarding their age, four of them were in 20's, seven of them were in 30's, seven of them were in 40's, and one of them was in 50's. As to marital status, twelve interviewees were married, and the other eight were still single. Seventeen were male, and three were female.

## Instrument

A semi-structured interview guide was developed based on our research aim and objectives, as well as literature review. An expert panel consisting of an associate professor in psychosocial rehabilitation, a professor in industrial/organizational psychology, a professor in nursing and a Ph.D. candidate in industrial/organizational psychology was set up to review the content validity, facial validity and linguistic smoothness of the interview guide. The final interview guide included two sections. The first section included 14 open-ended questions which investigated the possible factors contributing to the onset of depression in the workplace, such as daily life stressors, work stressors, attributors of stressors, coping strategies, stress reactions (to self, to productivity), practical and psychological influences of work to non-work areas, etc. The second section was on the demographic information, including gender, age, education level, work tenure, marriage status, and job

## Data Collection

Interviews were conducted according to standard methodology, including the use of trained interviewer, semi-structured interview guide, open-ended answers, audiotapes, interview transcriptions, and trained content analysts. Five pilot interviews were conducted to revise and finalize the interview guide. Each semi-structured interview was conducted in the place convenient to the subjects which was quiet, comfortable, and had no interruption such as the psychosocial laboratory of the Department of Rehabilitation Sciences at The Hong Kong Polytechnic University. Informed consent was sought prior to the interview. Each interview was transcribed by a Cantonese speaker with a background in rehabilitation.

## Data Analysis

The semi-structured interview data was analyzed by the content analysis approach. The contents of the semi-structured interviews were transcribed by a qualified research assistant who is also Cantonese speaker. Transcriptions were then used to generate coding categories and in turn to identify theories (Featherstone and Donovan, 1998; Brown and Lloyd, 2001; Griffee, 2005). According to the questions in interview guide, transcripts were analyzed by a series of stages to identify themes from the data. Five transcripts were randomly selected to develop the general codebook (GC) and attribution codebook (AC). GC was a codebook for all relevant themes except attributors of work stress which were coded in the AC. Two researchers independently conducted a thematic analysis of two transcripts by preliminary GC and AC. The consistent rates on GC between them were 80% and 88% for each transcript. Inconsistent coding items were discussed between the two coders under the supervision of the Project Leader till consensus was reached. The preliminary GC was revised according to pilot coding. Two another transcripts were randomly selected and coded independently again to check the inter-coder reliability. The consistent rates were 87.88% and 92.96% for each transcript.

For the AC, two transcripts were randomly selected and coded independently with the preliminary AC. The consistent rates for AC were 89.67% and 85.85% respectively. Each inconsistent coding was discussed between the coders under the supervision of the Project Leader till consensus was reached. No further revision of the preliminary AC was made.

Transcripts left were coded using the final GC and AC by one randomly selected coder. Code items with frequency lower than 4 were then sorted and grouped in case there were overlapping code items independently by two coders. Inconsistent sorting was discussed till consensus was reached.

# RESULTS

## Relevant Work Stressors

Frequency of code items on work stressors is shown in Table 2. Our result showed that the main work stressors endorsed by our interviewees were high demand on job performance, market fluctuation, work overtime/long work time, bad relationship with colleagues, high self-demands on work abilities, no allowance for making mistakes, time pressure, clients' complaint, and high competition.

## Attribution Processes for Work Stressors

Our participants were asked about their attribution for every work stressor they reported. The attributors were all sorted in terms of the work stressor so that every work stressor had different set of attributors. But if different stressors had a same attributor, this attributor would appear under each of those stressors.

## Table 2. Work Stressors in Financial Services Sector

| Work Stressors in Financial Services Sector | Frequency |
|---|---|
| High demand on job performance | 18 |
| Market fluctuation | 14 |
| Work overtime/long work time | 14 |
| Bad relationship with colleagues | 13 |
| High self-demands on work abilities | 12 |
| No allowance for making mistakes | 11 |
| Time pressure | 10 |
| Clients' complaint | 10 |
| High competition | 10 |
| Lack or loss of clients | 9 |
| Unsmooth career development | 9 |
| Communication problems with clients | 9 |
| Giving investment advice to clients | 8 |
| Intensive workload in certain moments or a short period | 8 |
| Sense of responsibility to clients | 7 |
| Low or unstable salary | 7 |
| Non-scheduled work/flow emergency work/always standing by | 7 |
| Clients' low credibility or disobeying rules | 6 |
| The need to maintain a good status and professional service attitudes all the time | 6 |
| Unlimited amount of market information | 6 |
| Bad relationship with supervisor | 5 |
| The need to adopt different ways of communication in terms of different | 5 |
| Interest conflicts between client and company | 5 |
| Maintenance of client relationship | 5 |
| High job turnover rate | 4 |
| Big variety of clients' requests | 4 |
| Organization atmosphere too money/performance-oriented | 4 |
| The need to figure out various methods on sales/marketing | 4 |
| Non-cooperation of supportive departments | 4 |
| Not being able to cope with the big variety of job demands | 4 |

As to main attributors of work stressors, we firstly picked up attributors with an endorsement rate at 25% or above. In the light of well-proved dimensions of cognitive attribution process (i.e., stability, globality, internality, controllability, intentionality) (Metalsky, Halberstadt, and Abramson, 1987; Abramson, Metalsky and Alloy, 1989), we sorted those main attributors again. It was found that main attributors were mostly on aspects as follows: Occupational and job intrinsic factors such as targeted markets being 24-hour operation or international, time being money, a close and direct relationship with changes or influences in economic environment, a high competitive atmosphere in financial industry, etc.; the uncontrollability of external economic environment, such as uncontrollable markets with unpredictable trend of stock price, low season, or bad market situation, etc.; the global influences of negative outcome, such as the need to compensate for loss with personal money, less time with family, client's complaints, boss's scolding, etc.; internal reasons such as lack of work experience and work ability, strong desire for self-accomplishment, effort, making mistake, etc.; people's intentionality such as incompliance of clients to rules, different working styles and ways of colleagues, demanding boss, etc.

### Table 3. Stress Coping Strategies of Financial Services Workers

| Stress Coping Strategies | Frequency |
|---|---|
| Entertainment activities | 14 |
| Seeking for family support | 14 |
| Changing attitudes/perception toward stressful/difficult situations | 12 |
| Distracting attention from work to non-work aspects | 10 |
| Strategic or cunning communication | 10 |
| Analyzing and solving problems | 9 |
| Taking initiative to improve cooperation or relationship | 9 |
| Sharing with colleagues | 8 |
| Considering job turnover or quitting job, or giving up promotion | 8 |
| Preparing well or practicing in advance to strengthen own abilities | 8 |
| Regulating mood so as not to influence work | 8 |
| Seeking for friends' support | 7 |
| Sports or exercises | 7 |
| Positively facing and managing stress | 7 |
| Making emergency plans | 6 |
| Sleep | 6 |
| Trying to get used to stress | 6 |
| learning lectures and experiences to improve | 6 |
| Being more careful at work | 5 |
| Eating | 5 |
| Ruminating problems/difficulties | 5 |
| Accepting the reality and thinking of it as a feature of this occupation | 5 |
| Drinking | 5 |
| Reading | 5 |
| Looking for other methods to solve problems | 5 |
| Going for vacation | 4 |
| Avoiding having family members share work stress | 4 |
| Thinking from the other side's perspective so as to understand his/her behaviors, becoming more tolerant | 4 |
| Traveling | 4 |
| Thinking about good sides | 4 |
| Being more motivated to work hard to solve the problem | 4 |
| Working under a controllable way by myself | 4 |

## Stress Coping Strategies

Stress coping strategies of our interviewees are presented in Table 3. The main strategies included entertainment activities (e.g., watching TV, movie), seeking for family support, changing own attitude and perception to difficulty and attitude, distracting self from work to non-work areas,, and strategic communication.

## Reactions to Stress

In response to work stressors in financial services sector, main stress reactions, as shown in the endorsement rate of our interviewees (>50%), were unhappy and tired. 40% of our interviewees had different kinds of sleep problems. 30% of our interviewees felt hardy, nervous and different kinds and different extent of pain such as stomachache, headache, toothache, eye-ache, etc. 25% of our interviewees felt exhausted and distracted or annoyed to different degree. 20% of our interviewees felt anxious in the wake of stress.

In regard to impairments of high work stress to productivity, being confronted with high work stress, at least half of our interviewees felt their work ability (e.g., decision making and judgment, work efficiency) was impaired, they were more inclined to make mistake, and they can't concentrate on their work. Table 4 shows the impairments to productivity of Financial Services Workers.

### Table 4. Impairments to Productivity of Financial Services Workers

| Impairments to Productivity | Frequency |
|---|---|
| Work ability decreasing (e.g., work efficiency, judgment, decision-making, etc.) | 12 |
| Inclination to make mistakes | 11 |
| absent-minded/not being able to concentrate on work | 10 |
| Lack of passion for work (e.g., no mood to work, low morale, reluctant to input effort, etc.) | 9 |
| Being more motivated to work hard | 6 |
| Communication ability lowering | 4 |

## Influences of Work Stress to Non-Work Areas

With respect to the influences of work stress to other life areas of financial services workers, it could be categorized into two areas: practical influence and attitudinal influence. Practical influences included long work time, lack of time being with family, health condition becoming worse, social life decrease, and lack of personal relaxation time. As to spiritual influence, most of our interviewees admitted after working in financial service sector for several years, they became more instrumental but cherished their family as well as friends more than before. Frequency of code items on practical influences and attitudinal influences are shown in Table 5 and Table 6 respectively.

## Table 5. Practical Influences

| Practical Influences | Frequency |
|---|---|
| Work overtime/long work time | 13 |
| Lack of time being with family | 13 |
| Social life reducing | 10 |
| Lack of personal relaxation time | 10 |
| Health condition deteriorating | 10 |
| No more energy to do other things due to most of energy being occupied by work | 9 |
| Taking work home | 8 |
| Becoming bad-tempered | 8 |
| Mood become easily influenced by work | 7 |
| Lack of sleep | 7 |
| The need to help friends invest | 5 |
| Lack of time to implement responsibility for family (e.g., taking care of kids or old parents) | 5 |
| Becoming more knowledgeable, experiences and mature | 5 |
| Lack of time to do exercises | 5 |
| The need to use private resources to attain work target | 4 |
| Mental status becoming worse | 4 |

## Table 6. Attitudinal Influences

| Attitudinal Influences | Frequency |
|---|---|
| Becoming more instrumental | 18 |
| Cherishing family and friends more | 12 |
| Becoming indifferent to fame and gain and less instrumental | 7 |
| Learning to accept and feel content about present life and reality | 6 |
| Only endeavor is useless to obtaining success | 6 |
| It's very difficult to make money | 5 |
| Stress is an impetus of improvement | 5 |
| People working in financial area can't be trusted | 5 |
| Attaching more importance to health | 4 |
| Becoming more pessimistic to an individual's strength to be against/solve stressful/aversive situations | 4 |
| Emotion should be controlled | 4 |

## Possible Ways for Management Level to Improve those Stressful Situations

In our interview, we also collected interviewees' opinions about ways to improve their stressful situations. In descending order, their suggestions are improving the communication with employees and among employees, improving management (e.g., improving the efficiency of work procedure and organizational institutions, multitasking, organizational fairness, leadership, teamwork, etc.), improving organization atmosphere to make it more care about its employees, more humanistic, more altruistic, and more trusting, improving work abilities of employees (e.g., on customer relationship and communication, time management, stress management, etc.) and organizing more relaxing activities to release worker's stress. Frequencies of above codes are shown in Table 7.

**Table 7. Possible Ways for Management Level to Improve Stressful Situations**

| Possible Ways for Management Level | Frequency |
|---|---|
| Improving the communication with employees and among employees | 8 |
| Improving organizational management | 8 |
| Improving organization atmosphere to make it more care about its employees, more humanistic, more altruistic, and more trusting | 7 |
| Improving employees' work abilities | 5 |
| Organizing more relaxing activities to release worker's stress | 5 |

## DISCUSSION

Our result shows that workers in financial services industry generally perceive their work stress as heavy and mainly from high demand on work performance (e.g., high sales figure or quota for commission), market fluctuation, long work time, bad relationship with colleagues, high self-demand on work ability, no allowance for making mistakes, time pressure, client's complaint, and high competition. As attributed by financial services workers themselves, those main stressors in their workplace are characterized by uncontrollability, unpredictability, occurring cyclically, and unmanageable people's intention. For example, the situation of financial markets were considered uncontrollable when it's in low season bad situations, stock price was considered unpredictable, stress of job intrinsic factors were considered occurring cyclically, you can't manage client's incompliance to rules, and so on. All those features made workers in financial services sector vulnerable to depression (Abramson, Alloy, and Hankin, 2002).

Therefore, when it comes to stress coping strategies, most of them, illustrated by our result, were focused on themselves. In other words, because of the difficulty in changing their particular work environment, the only thing they can do to release their work stress is adjusting themselves emotionally and cognitively to those stressful situations or just avoiding those distressing situations. However, there is a study suggesting that only adapting and adjusting workers to stressful situations instead of changing their environmental factors coordinately, also a way usually adopted by present popular stress management programs, can not contribute to improving worker's well-being significantly (Cooper et al., 2001). Considering that, and together with the high stressful work environment confronting financial services workers, their well-being is really a pressing problem that needs to be addressed.

In terms of stress reactions, our result shows that most workers in financial services sectors feel unhappy and tired, and are suffering some extent of sleep problems as well as different kinds of somatic discomforts such as stomachache and headache, which are all symptoms of burnout and depression (APA, 1994). Moreover, these may lead to impairments o work abilities or productivity caused by particular stressors such as decision and judgment ability decrease, inclination of making mistakes and problem in concentration are concerned with symptoms of burnout and depression (Lerner et al., 2004; Stewart et al., 2003).

Our results show that the respondents' work interfere with their family life, social life, and health condition as well as personal life, which are all important life areas. This interference is particularly severe to those workers who have to take care of kids or parents. As shown in our result, this exerts great harm to workers' psychological well-being (Ford, Heinen, Langkamer, 2007). On the other hand, experiences in the workplace also have negative influence on their attitudes toward non-work areas. They became more instrumental when dealing with their life, which is not good for their emotional well-being and in turn impairs their psychological well-being.

Taken together, we noticed a great susceptibility of workers in financial services sector to depression, and this qualitative study also reveals some crucial factors which may contribute to depressive symptoms among those workers.

# DIRECTIONS FOR FURTHER STUDY

## Questionnaire Development

Based on our results, we may construct two questionnaires, one to measure specific work stress of workers in financial services sector and another to measure their attribution style. These two questionnaires are very important instruments to investigate possible factors and mechanisms contributing to depressive symptoms of financial services workers (FSW).

In our future study, we will base on the results of this phase of study to compile Perceived Stress Questionnaire for FSW and Attribution Style Questionnaire for FSW, and use them as instruments to investigate possible etiologies of depression among financial services workers.

## Quantitative Study to Verify Possible Etiologies of Depression

This qualitative study revealed some possible factors accounting for depressive symptoms among workers in financial services sectors. The results will serve the foundation of further quantitative research to verify those factors disclosed in the qualitative study. For future study, follow-up survey could be used to identify underlying causal relationships among those factors relevant to the onset of depressive symptoms among financial services workers.

## Study on Rehabilitation of Workers with Depressive Symptoms

Based on the factors and mechanisms which precipitate depressive symptoms of workers identified in preceding research, we could develop a rehabilitative program to help those workers alleviate their symptoms by integrating psychosocial treatments of depression with existing programs of stress management (e.g., Employee Assistance Program) in organizations, and meanwhile, intervene in their work environment through a series of management policies that target to improve those harmful organizational or job intrinsic factors.

## Study on other Occupations

Based on similar methodology we used in this study, further research could be conducted to find out the factors precipitating depression in other occupations such as doctors, nurses, teachers, and lawyers.

## REFERENCES

Abramson, L. Y., Alloy, L. B., and Hankin, B. L. (2002). Cognitive vulnerability-stress models of depression in a self-regulatory and psychobiological context. In I. H. Gotlib and C. L. Hammen (Eds.), *Handbook of Depression* (pp. 268-294). New York: Guilford Press.

Abramson, L.Y., Metalsky, G.I., and Alloy, L.B. (1989). Hopelessness Depression: A theory-based subtype of depression. *Psychological Review*, 96, 358-372.

Ahola, K., Honkonen, T., Isometsa, E., Kalimo, R., Nvkvri, E., Aromaa, A., and Lonngvist, J. (2005). The relationship between job-related burnout and depressive disorders—results from the Finnish Health 2000 Study. *Journal of Affective Disorders,* 88(1), 55-62.

American Psychiatric Association. (1994). *Diagnostic and Statistical Manual of Mental Disorders* (4th ed.). Washington, D.C.: American Psychiatric Association.

Bakker, A.B., Schaufeli, W.B., Demerouti, E., Janssen, P.M.P., Van der Hulst, R., and Brouwer, J. (2000). Using equity theory to examine the difference between burnout and depression. *Anxiety Stress Coping,* 13, 247-268.

Barge-Schaapveld, D. (1999). Quality of life in depression: daily life determinants and variability. *Psychiatry Research,* 88 (3), 173-189.

Barlow, D.H., and Durand, V.M. (1995). *Abnormal Psychology: an integrative approach.* Brooks/Cole Publishing Company, Pacific Grove, California.

Beck, A. T. (1983). Cognitive therapy of depression: New perspectives. In P. J. Clayton and J. E. Barrett (Eds.), *Treatment of depression: Old controversies and new approaches* (pp. 265-290). New York: Raven Press.

Beck, A. T. (1987). Cognitive models of depression. *Journal of Cognitive Psychotherapy: An International Quarterly,* 1, 5-37.

Beck, A. T. (1996). Beyond belief: A theory of modes, personality and psychopathology. In P. M. Salkovskis (Ed.), *Frontiers of cognitive therapy* (pp. 1-25). New York: Guilford Press.

Beekman, A.T.F., de Beurs, E., van Balkom, A.J.L.M., Deeg, D.J.H., van Dyck, R., and van Tilburg, W. (2000). Anxiety and depression in later life: Co-occurrence and communality of risk factors. *American Journal of Psychiatry,* 157, 89-95.

Bell, R.B., Davison, M., and Sefcik, D. (2002). A first surveymeasuring burnout in emergency medicine physician assistants. *Journal of the American Academy of Physician Assistants,* 15(3), 40–55.

Berndt, E. R., Finkelstein, S. N., Greenberg, P. E., et al. (1998). Workplace performance effects from chronic depression and its treatment. *Journal of Health Economy,* 17, 511-535.

Blatt, S.J., D'Afflitti, J.P., and Quinlan, D.M. (1976). Experiences of depression in normal young adults. *Journal of Abnormal Psychology,* 85, 383-389

Blatt, S.J., and Shichman, S. (1983). Two primary configurations of psychopathology. *Psychoanalysis and Contemporary Thought,* 6, 187-254.

Blatt, S.J., and Zuroff, D.C. (1992). Interpersonal relatedness and self-definition: Two prototypes for depression. *Clinical Psychology Review,* 12, 527-562

B.L.S. (2003). Census of fatal occupational injuries. Fatal injuries. Washington, DC: U.S. Department of Labor, Bureau of Labor Statistics, Safety and Health Statistics Program. www.bls.gov/iif/oshcfoi1.htm

Bluen, S.D., Barling, J., and Burns, W. (1990). Predicting sales performance, job satisfaction, and depression by using the achievement strivings and impatience-irritability dimensions of type A behavior. *Journal of Applied Psychology,* 75(2), 212-216.

Brenninkmeyer, V., Van Yperen, N.W., and Buunk, B.P. (2001). Burnout and depression are not identical twins: is decline of superiority a distinguishing feature? *Personality and Individual Differences, 30,* 873-880.

Brown, C., and Lloyd-Jones, T.J. (2001). Verbalization may interfere with or facilitate multiple face recognition. *British Psychological Society, Cognitive Section, Edinburgh, September.*

Burke, R.J., and Greenglass, E.R. (2001). Hospital restructuring and nursing staff well-being: The role of perceived hospital and union support. *Anxiety, stress and coping, 14,* 93-115.

Cable, D.M., and DeRue, S. (2002). The construct, convergent, and discriminant validity of subjective fit perceptions. *Journal of Applied Psychology,* 87, 875–884.

Cable, D. M., and Edwards, J. R. (2004). Complementary and discriminant validity of subjective fit perceptions. *Journal of Applied Psychology,* 87(5), 875-884.

Cass, A. (2000). A study finds depression and stress common among successful young brokers. *On Wall Street,* August 2000, 31-32.

Cooper, C.L., and Marshall, J. (1976). Occupational sources of stress: review of literature relating to coronary heart disease and mental ill health. *Journal of Occupational Psychology,* 49, 11-28

Cooper, C.L., Dewe, P.J., and O'Driscoll, M.P. (2001). *Organizational stress: A review and critique of theory, research and applications.* United Kingdom: Sage Publications.

Cox, T., and Mackay, C. (1981). A transactional approach to occupational stress. In Corlett and Richardson, *Work design and productivity.* Wiley and Sons: Chichester.

Coyne, J.C., and Whiffen, V.E. (1995). Issues in personality as diathesis for depression: the case of sociotropy-dependency and autonomy-self-criticism. *Psychological Bulletin,* 118(3), 358-378.

Daniels, K., and Guppy, A. (1997). Stressors, locus of control, and social support as consequences of affective psychological well-being. *Journal of Occupational Health Psychology,* 2, 156-174.

Demerouti, E., Bakker, A.B., Nachreiner, F., Schaufeli, W.B. (2001). The job demands-resources model of burnout. *Journal of Applied Psychology,* 86(3), 499-512.

de Lange, A. H., Taris, T. W., Houtman, I. L. D., and Bongers, P. M. (2003). "The very best of the millennium": Longitudinal research and the demand-control-(support) model. *Journal of Occupational Health Psychology*, 8, 282-305.

Desjarlais, R., Eisenberg, L., Good, B., and Kleinman, A. (1995). *World mental health: Problems and priorities in low income countries.* New York, Oxford: Oxford University Press.

Dewa, C.S., and Lin, E. (2000). Chronic physical illness, psychiatric disorder and disability in the workplace. *Social Science and Medicine,* 51, 41-50.

Edwards, J.R., and Cooper, C.L. (1990). The person-environment fit approach to stress: Recurring problems and some suggested solutions. *Journal of Organizational Behavior,* 10, 293-307.

Edwards, J. R. (1991). Person-job fit: A conceptual integration, literature review, and methodological critique. *International Review of Industrial and Organizational Psychology, 6,* 283–357.

Edwards, J.R. (1996). An examination of competing versions of the person-environment fit approach to stress. *Academy of Management Journal,* 39(2), 292-339.

Edwards, J.R., and Pothbard, N.P. (2000). Mechanisms linking work and family: Clarifying the relationship between work and family constructs. *Academy of Management Review,* 25(1), 178-199.

Eysenck, H.J. (1968). *Eysenck Personality Inventory (Manual).* San Diego, Educational and Industrial Testing Service.

Featherstone, K., and Donovan, J. L. (1998). Random allocation or allocation at random? Patients' perspectives of participation in a randomised controlled trial. *British Medical Journal*, 317, 1177-1180.

Ford, M.T., Heinen, B.A., and Langkamer, K.L. (2007). Work and family satisfaction and conflict: A meta-analysis of cross-domain relations. *Journal of Applied Psychology,* 92(1), 57-80.

Friedman, M. and Rosenman, R. H. (1974). *Type A behavior and your heart.* New York: Knopf.

Freudenberger, H.J. (1975). The staff burnout syndrome in alternative institutions. *Psychother. Theory Res. Pract, 12,* 72-83.

Glass, D.C., and McKnight, J.D. (1996). Perceived control, depressive symptomatology, and professional burnout: A review of the evidence. *Psychology and Health,* 11, 23–48.

Griffee, D. T. (2005). Research Tips: Interview Data Collection. *Journal of Developmental Education, 28*(3), 36-7.

Grosch, J. W., and Murphy, L. R. (1998). Occupational differences in depression and global health: Results form a national sample of US workers. *Journal of Occupational Environmental Medicine*, 40, 153-164.

Hall, D.T., and Mansfield, R. (1971). Organizational and individual response to external stress. *Administrative Science Quarterly,* 16, 533-547.

Hockey, G.R.J. (1993). Cognitive-energetical control mechanisms in the management of work demands and psychological health. In A. Baddely and L. Weiskrantz (Eds.), *Attention: Selection, awareness, and control* (pp. 328-345). Oxford, England: Clarendon Press.

Iacovides, A., Fountoulakis, K.N., Kaprinis, S., and Kaprinis, G. (2003). The relationship between job stress, burnout and clinical depression. *Journal of Affect Disorder, 75(3)*, 209-221.

Ivancevich, J.M., and Matteson, M.T. (1980). *Stress and work.* Glenview, IL: Scott, Foresman.

Jansen, K. J., and Kristof-Brown, A.K. (2006). Toward a multidimensional theory of person-environment fit. *Journal of Management Issues, 18*, 193-212.

Jenkins, R., Lewis, G., Bebbington, P., Brugha, T., Farrell, M., and Gill, B. (1997). The National Psychiatric Morbidity Surveys of Great Britain: Initial findings from the Household Survey. *Psychological Medicine, 27*, 775-89.

Johnson, P., and Indvik, J. (1997). The boomer blues: Depression in the workplace. *Public Personnel Management, 26*, 359-365.

Judge, T.A., and Cable, D.M. (1997). Applicant personality, organizational culture, and organization attraction. *Personnel Psychology, 50(2)*, 359-394.

Karasek, R. A. (1979). Job demands, job control, and mental strain: Implications for job redesign. *Administrative Science Quarterly, 24*, 285-308.

Karasek, R. A., and Theorell, T. (1990). *Healthy work: Stress, productivity, and the reconstruction of working life.* New York: Basic Books.

Kobasa, S.C., Maddi, S.R., and Kahn, S. (1982). Hardiness and health: A prospective study. *Journal of Personality and Social Psychology, 42(1)*, 168-177.

Kristof, A. L. (1996). Person–organization fit: an integrative review of its conceptualizations, measurement, and implications. *Personnel Psychology, 49*, 1–49.

Kristof-Brown, A. L. (2000). Perceived applicant fit: Distinguishing between recruiters' perceptions of person-job and person-organization fit. *Personnel Psychology, 53*, 643–671.

Kristop-Brown, A. L., Zimmerman, R. D., and Johnson, E. C. (2005). Consequences of individuals' fit at work: A meta-analysis of person-job, person-organization, person-group, and person-supervisor fit. *Personnel Psychology, 58*, 281-342.

Lanier, E. (2003). Depression: The hidden workplace illness. *Professional Safety*, 48, 27-30.

Lazarus, R.S., and Folkman, S. (1984). *Stress, coping, and adaptation.* New York: Springer.

Lazarus, R.S., DeLongis, A., Folkman, S., and Gruen, R. (1985). Stress and adaptational outcomes: The problem of confounded measures. *American Psychologist*, 40, 770-779.

Leiter, M.P. and Durup, J. (1994). The discriminant validity of burnout and depression: A confirmatory factor analytic study. *Anxiety Stress Coping, 7*, 357-373.

Lerner, D., Adler, D. A., Chang, H., Berndt, E. R., Irish, J. T., Lapitsky, L., Hood, M. Y., Reed, J., and Rogers, W. H. (2004). The clinical and occupational correlates of work productivity loss among employed patients with depression. *Journal of Occupational and Environmental Medicine, 46*, 46-55.

Liu, P., and Van-Liew, D.A. (2003). Depression and burnout. In: J.P. Kahn, and A.M. Langlieb (Eds), *Mental health and productivity in the workplace: A handbook for organizations and clinicians* (pp. 433-457). San Francisco, CA, US: Jossey-Bass.

Maslach, C. (1976). Burned-out. *Human Behavior, 5*, 16-22.

Maslach, C., and Jackson, S.E. (1986). *Maslash Burnout Inventory manual* (2nd ed.). Palo Alto, CA: Consulting Psychologists Press.

Maslach, C., and Schaufeli, W.B. (1993). Historical and conceptual development of burnout. In W.B. Schaufeli, C. Maslach, and T. Marek (Eds.), *Professional burnout: Recent developments in theory and research* (pp. 1-16). Washington, DC: Taylor and Frances.

Maslach, C., and Leiter, M.P. (1997). *The truth about burnout.* San Francisco: Jossey-Bass.

Maslach, C., Schaufeli, W.B., and Leiter, M. P. (2001). *Job burnout. Annual Review of Psychology,* 52, 397-422.

Matteson, M. T., and Ivancevich, J. M. (1979). Organizational stressors and heart disease: A research model. *Academy of Management Review*, 4, 347-357.

McGrath, J.E. (1976). Stress and behavior in organizations. In M.D. Dunnette (Ed.), *Handbook of industrial and organizational psychology,* (pp. 1351-1396). Chicago: Rand McNally.

Metalsky, G.I., Halberstadt, L.J., and Abramson, L.Y. (1987). Vulnerability to depressive mood reactions: toward a more powerful test of the diathesis-stress and causal mediation components of the reformulated theory of depression. *Journal of Personality and Social Psychology,* 52(2), 386-393.

MHF. (2000). *The cost of mental health problems. The fundamental fact.* The Mental Health Foundation, UK, www.mentalhealth.org.uk//ffcost.html

Montgomery, D. C., Blodgett, J. G., and Barnes, J. H. (1996). A model of financial securities salespersons' job stress. *Journal of Services Marketing*, 10(3), 21-38.

Muchinsky, P.M., and Monahan, C.J. (1987). What is person-environment congruence? Supplementary versus complementary models of fit. *Journal of Vocational Behavior*, 31, 268-77.

Murray, K.B., and Schlacter, J.L. (1990). The Impact of Services Versus Goods on Consumers' Assessment of Perceived Risk and Variability. *Academy of Marketing Science Journal*, 18(1), 51-66.

NIDRR. (1993). *Strategies, employment, mental illness: strategies to secure and maintain employment for people with long-term mental illness.* United States National Institute on Disability and Ruehabilitation Research (NIDRR), XV (10).

National Institute for Occupational Safety and Health. (2004). *High-Risk Industries and Occupations.* Worker Health Chartbook, Chapter 3.

Nolen-Hoeksema, S. (1991). Responses to depression and their effects on the duration of depressive episodes. *Journal of Abnormal Psychology*, 100, 569-582.

Parker, D.F., and DeCotiis, T.A. (1983). Organizational determinants of job stress. *Organizational Behaviour and Human Performance,* 32, 160-177.

Pollard, T.M. (2001). Changes in mental well-being, blood pressure and total cholesterol levels during workplace reorganization: The impact of uncertainty. *Work and Stress*, 51, 14–28.

Richter, P., and Hacker, W. (1998). *Workload and strain: Stress, fatigue, and burnout in working life.* Heidelberg, Germany: Asagner.

Sadock, B.J. and Sadock, V.A. (2004). *Kaplan and Sadock's Comprehensive Textbook of Psychiatry* (8th ed.). Lippincott, Williams and Wilkins: Baltimore.

Saks, A. M., and Ashforth, B. E. (1997). A longitudinal investigation of the relationships between job information sources, applicant perceptions of fit, and work outcomes. *Personnel Psychology,* 50, 395–426.

Saks, A. M., and Ashforth, B. E. (2002). Is job search related to employment quality? It all depends on the fit. *Journal of Applied Psychology*, 87, 646–654.

Schwarz, N., and Clore, G.L. (2003). Mood as information: 20 years later. *Psychological Inquiry*, 14, 296-303.

Schaufeli, W.B., and Enzmann, D. (1998). *The burnout companion to study and practice: A critical analysis*. Philadelphia: Taylor and Francis.

Schneider, B. (2001). Fits about fit. *Applied Psychology: An International Review*, 50(1), 141–152.

Seligman, M.E.P. (1975). *Helplessness: On depression, development and death*. San Francisco: Freeman.

Shirom, A., and Ezrachi, Y. (2003). On the discriminant validity of burnout, depression and anxiety: A re-examination of the burnout measure. *Anxiety, Stress and Coping*, 16, 83-97.

Siegrist, J. (1996). Adverse health effects of high-effort/low-reward conditions. *Journal of Occupational Health Psychology*, 1(1), 27-41.

Siegrist, J. (2001). A theory of occupational stress. In J. Dunham (Ed.), *Stress in the workplace: Past, present and future* (pp. 52–66). London: Whurr Publishers, Ltd.

Siu, O. L., and Donald, I. (1996). Psychosocial factors at work and workers' health in Hong Kong: An exploratory study. *Bulletin of the Hong Kong Psychological Society January and July 1995*, 34/35, 30-56.

Spector, P.E. (1982) Behavior in organizations as a function. of employee's locus of control. *Psychological Bulletin*, 91(3),. 482–497.

Spector, P.E. (1988). Development of the Work Locus of Control Scale. *Journal of Occupational Psychology*, 61, 335-340.

Spector, P.E., and O'Connell, B.J. (1994). The contribution of personality traits, negative affectivity, locus of control and type A to the subsequent reports of job stressors and job strains. *Journal of Occupational and Organizational Psychology*, 67(1), 1-11.

STAKES. (1999). *Introduction to mental health issues in the EU*. Helsinki, Finnish Ministry of Social Affairs and Health, www.stakes.fi/mentalhealth

Stewart, W. F., Ricci, J. A., Chee, E., Hahn, S. R., and Morganstein, D. (2003). Cost of lost productive work time among US workers with depression. *Journal of the American Medical Association*, 289, 3135-3144.

Tennant, C. (2001). Work-related stress and depressive disorders. *Journal of Psychosomatic Research*, 51, 697-704.

Tsutsumi, A., and Kawakami, N. (2004). A review of empirical studies on the model of effort-reward imbalance at work: reducing occupational stress by implementing a new theory. *Social Science and Medicine*, 59(1), 2335-2359.

UKDH. (1993). *Mental illness: key area handbook. The health of the nation*. London, UK Department of Health, 11-24.

van der Doef, M. P., and Maes, S. (1999). The job demand-control(-support) model and psychological well-being: A review of 20 years of empirical research. *Work and Stress*, 13, 87-114.

WHO., and ILO. (2000). *Mental health and work: Impact, issues and good practices*. Geneva: World Health Organization and International Labor Organization.

WHO. (1992). *The ICD-10 Classification of Mental and Behavioral Disorders*. Geneva: World Health Organization.

WHO. (2001). *The World Health Report: 2001: Mental Health: New Understanding.* New Hope. Geneva: World Health Organization.

Ylipaavalniemi, J., Kivimlki, M., Elovainia, M., Virtanen, M., Keltikangas-Jlrvinen, L., and Vahtera, J. (2005). Psychosocial work characteristics and incidence of newly diagnosed depression: a prospective cohort study of three different models. *Social Science and Medicine,* 61, 111-122.

Zubin, J., and Spring, B. (1977). Vulnerability: A new view of schizophrenia. *Journal of Abnormal Psychology,* 86, 103-126.

Zuroff, D. C., Mongrain, M., and Santor, D. A. (2004). Conceptualizing and measuring personality vulnerability to depression: Comment on Coyne and Whiffen (1995). *Psychological Bulletin,* 130, 489-511.

In: Industrial Psychology Research Trends
Editor: Ina M. Pearle, pp. 73-87

ISBN: 978-1-60021-825-5
© 2007 Nova Science Publishers, Inc.

*Chapter 4*

# FUEL WASTING BEHAVIORS OF TRUCK DRIVERS

## *A. E. af Wåhlberg*[*1] *and J. Göthe*[2]

[1] Department of Psychology; Uppsala University, Sweden
[2] VDI Innovation AB

## ABSTRACT

The driving behavior of most drivers is sub-optimal concerning fuel consumption. However, little is known of how important different sources of waste are in terms of how common such behavior is on the road. This question was studied in a small sample of logging truck drivers for the variables idling, high speed, shifting gear, rpm and braking, with various statistical methods. In multiple regressions it was found that the studied factors explained a large part of the existing variance. Also, the ranking of the studied factors as to their relative importance as sources of waste differed depending on the method of analysis used, indicating that exactly how the question is put to the same data can shape the answer. The results have implications for training of drivers in fuel-efficient driving, as well as for the development of support tools and driving cycles.

**Keywords:** fuel consumption, driver behavior, feedback.

## INTRODUCTION

During the last decades of the 20th century, interest in various ways of saving fuel was mounting, while transports proliferated. Meanwhile, it was found that various driving related behaviors could be changed in the direction of less consumption (e.g. Runnion, Watson, & McWorther, 1978; Rothstein, 1980; Siero, Boon, Kok & Siero, 1989), although maybe not for very long time periods. Also, scattered reports indicated that prodigious amounts of fuel was

* Corresponding author : Box 1225; S-751 42 Uppsala, Sweden; e-mail: anders.af_wahlberg@psyk.uu.se; Homepage: http://www.psyk.uu.se/hemsidor/busdriver/ index.htm; Tel: +46-18-471 25 90, +46-18-33 50 95; Fax: +46-18-471 21 23

wasted due to driver behavior in terms of driving style, and that this too could be changed (e.g. Laurell, 1985; Nader, 1991). In the wake of this, a number of organizations and companies started marketing economical driving (see www.ecodrive.org; Govaerts & Verlaak, 2003). However, although the effects during training often are in the range of 10-15 percent reduction (Laurell, 1985; af Wåhlberg, 2002), it is uncertain how this transfers to normal driving over longer time periods, as very little longitudinal research has been undertaken (af Wåhlberg, 2002). Mainly, the results seem to be of a very small effect (af Wåhlberg, 2006; in press). It has also been found that people may have difficulties in understanding and applying written information about how to drive, resulting in erroneous behavior (van de Burgwal & Gense, 2002).

An alternative (or rather a complement) to ecodriving training is various types of technical feedback systems, of which a number have been marketed in the first years of the 21st century. They can roughly be divided into three categories according to what kind of information is provided; fuel consumption meters, driving behavior meters, and driving tips apparatus. The first is for example the in-vehicle computer that is standard in many vehicles produced today, yielding information about the fuel consumed momentarily, or for the last trip etc. The second measures some aspect of driver behavior other than the overall fuel consumption, with the 'green area' of rpm-meters as a primitive example. Finally, direct advice on what to do may be given (e.g. 'shift gear'). In reality, these categories often co-exist within one apparatus.

So far, there seems to be virtually no research at all on how drivers react to feedback on fuel consumption in a longitudinal perspective (apart from af Wåhlberg, in press), although similar setups for general driving style have been found to reduce accident frequency (Wouters & Bos, 2000). Three main possibilities would seem to exist; drivers can ignore the feedback, they can learn a new driving style so thoroughly that they do not need the extra information (instead relying on speed, vibrations etc), or they can rely on the feedback to provide necessary information.

However, there would seem to exist one basic lack of information which precedes even the construction of feedback apparatus; even though it is possible to list the possible unnecessary losses of energy in a vehicle due to driver behavior (braking, sub optimal acceleration etc) and construct some type of feedback concerning these variables, this does not mean that the problem is actually present out on the road. This problem would seem to be similar for driving cycles; are the assumptions underpinning their construction representative for the driver behavior they are supposed to simulate? For feedback apparatus construction and development of training, the question might be put as 'Do we target the most important parts of behavior for this driver population?'. It might be added that during training in EcoDriving, the teacher assesses each pupil individually to be able to alter the most important errors committed. This type of individual tailoring, however, is not only dependent on the subjective views of the instructor[1], it is usually not possible to achieve with technical feedback systems, as they are fixed as to their type of information; they cannot rank importance of different behaviors, or most often not even measure them.

---

[1] Unless he/she has the kind of fuel consumption meter that can measure different parts of driver fuel wasting behavior.

When driving a vehicle, a large part of the fuel is wasted, if 'wasted' is defined as not used for actually moving the vehicle (overcoming friction). These behaviors include;

- braking (the energy produced from the fuel is lost)
- idling (no work is produced)
- gear changing (the engine runs while the clutch is not engaged)
- high speed (air resistance increase with an exponential rate)

Two things should be fairly obvious from this description; that all these components are to a large part under the influence of driver behavior, and that their relative importance will change between different people, vehicles, loads and roads. For example, buses for public transport in city environments will probably use no extra fuel due to high speeds, but a large amount for accelerating after (unnecessary) braking.

Although it would in theory be possible to achieve very high efficiency in driving, and several studies have shown that it is possible to teach drivers to drive in more efficient ways (e.g. Laurell, 1985; Nader, 1991; af Wåhlberg, 2002) this is obviously not the state of the art out in the daily traffic. The study of what behaviors exist 'out there' is therefore obviously of some importance, for example for the development of driving cycles, teaching of driving technique and feedback devices.

However, it would still be rather uncertain exactly how common fuel wasting behaviors of different sorts are, or their relative importance. As fuel consumption is an overall measure, this question cannot be answered by raw consumption. Neither is it possible to simulate or test this in a laboratory, unless you have exact and representative data on human behavior and traffic environments etc. Getting such data would still need field investigations, and it would thus be easier to measure the different fuel wasting behaviors directly, given that you can calculate how fuel is used for the different purposes described above.

Such apparatus is now in existence, and a project was conceived with the main object of studying if it was possible to influence driver behavior with advanced instantaneous and long-term feedback on various aspects of fuel consumption. This equipment (described in detail below) uses engine and vehicle data to, amongst other things, calculate the fuel spent on the a) to d) factors described above (which make it very similar to the tool developed by van der Voort, Dougherty and van Maarseveen, 2001). However, as an aside of this project, it would seem to be possible to study the problem of the relative importance of the various fuel wasting behaviors in this population, which became the focus of the present paper.

Technicians have a vast knowledge about vehicles, engines and fuel consumption, while traffic psychologists have started to work on driver behavior in its interaction with these factors. But while technicians seem to prefer mathematical formulas for the description of data, psychologists mainly use inference techniques to decide how good an approximation of the population values they have achieved. In the twilight land between human behavior and technology, it would seem to be necessary to use both these ways of analysis to ascertain if they are reliable tools.

However, it could be suspected that different mathematical methods would yield different answers to the question of relative importance of fuel wasting behavior. In the present study, the main task set out is to sort the five factors noted above (plus one non-driving factor) as to their relative importance for fuel consumption. But what is deemed 'important' may differ, and the type of analysis chosen will be a reflection of this choice. Therefore, the answer to the question of relative importance will partly be determined by how the question is put. In the present paper, some different techniques will be compared, and the answers they yield discussed.

A very basic way of assessing the importance of driver behaviors is to calculate the percent that they add to the total. This method will actually indicate the absolute, raw amount of fuel spent in different ways. However, it will not say anything about how much of an effect the behavior studied has when it is present. Phrased another way, a behavior might have a very large effect (spend a lot of fuel when it is utilized) but be rare, and thus not spend much energy in total. It might then be asked whether it would be easier to target for change a common behavior that spend little fuel when present, or the uncommon high-waste behavior?

A different way of calculating importance is by way of correlations. Here, a measure is given that indicates how well one variable might be predicted from another, which in this case would be the total fuel consumption on a trip from, for example, idling. Prediction, however, is one thing, the amount of change in variable with the other quite another. The latter is instead given by the regression equation of the correlation. With this method, one might therefore see how well each of the fuel wasting behaviors stated above correspond to the total, and how much they contribute. However, there is a drawback of this method; the predictor variables may very well be intercorrelated, and thus indicate something that is not really true, i.e. you would get to much variance explained.

The statistical technique of choice for psychologists in multivariate studies is therefore often multiple regression analysis. This least-squares method calculates the unique contribution of each independent variable for the prediction of the dependent (thus negating the influence of intercorrelations), as well as the slope of the regression line for each of these associations, and a number of other coefficients. As the data in this study had the form of the total fuel consumption on a trip, as well as the amount spent on the a) to d) factors, this type of analysis would seem to be appropriate. Used on the present data, it utilizes the variance in fuel consumption as well as waste behaviors between trips to ascertain how each factor contributes. The results will therefore show how much of the variance in fuel consumption is explained by waste behaviors, and how strongly such behaviors influence the consumption, two things which are very different. The latter means that a factor might have a strong effect whenever it is present, but the first will show in what amount it is actually present. Thus, in theory, a major factor in an engineering calculation might turn out to be insignificant, because the behavior is not present, and vice versa.

It should be noted that the present approach to data is different from standard psychological studies as it uses one drive (a 'trip') as the unit of analysis instead of the individual. N will therefore become very large, which is essential for the use of multiple regression. It might also be added that the use of a different mathematical method as compared to those used in the measurement equipment lends some independency to the results.

Summing up, the main research questions of the present work were;

- what are the relative importance of the a) to d) fuel consumption factors described above for the type of driving studied?
- do different mathematical methods yield the same answers?

- tentatively (due to the very small sample of drivers used), are there apparent differences in importance of factors between drivers?
- noting how much variance the measured driver errors can explain in total fuel consumption, i.e. how much there is left for other factors.

# METHOD

## General

Data was gathered as part of a project on fuel-efficient driving. The drivers used the technical feedback equipment DV4 (see Appendix and the next section) in their normal work. Apart from instantaneous feedback on their behavior, overall results for each driver was delivered by mail every two weeks, and discussed with the drivers' closest superior.

## Technical Equipment: The VDI Innovation Feedback System

The VDI Innovation product is based on a software program that, via CAN and the FMS-protocol or J1708, deliver highly detailed information on multiple factors concerning fuel consumption and other data of interest such as, for example, the total amount of exhaust emissions, divided between 'during transport', 'idling' and 'PTO[2] work'. The DV4 can also calculate the lowest possible consumption at any given time and simultaneously read the actual amount of fuel used, thus showing how much is 'wasted'. Further, it can identify the behaviors that increase the fuel consumption, like brake use, speed, gearshift, gear work and idling. As of that, the company or instructors can give the driver clear instructions on what can be done to limit the overuse based on the individual driver's behavior. The concept also includes a course for the driver that aims to teach the basic concepts of driving as economically as possible. This includes trying to use the engine braking power as much as possible instead of the brake pedal. Not only does this lead to softer decelerations, but also a total shutoff of diesel supply to the engine. The distance for shutoff therefore becomes an important indicator of economical driving.

With a GSM connection, the DV4 can send the gathered information to a server and let customers access an interface for statistics and reports. A handheld computer unit (PDA) is installed in the cabin so that the driver can access and view reports. The driver also gets real time feedback on fuel consumption and suggestions on when to shift gears.

It should be pointed out that the measurements of fuel consumption versus other variables use independent sources of information from the vehicle. The first is calculated by the vehicle computer (CAN system) from the fuel injection system, while all the other are products of various sensors and the DV4.

---

[2] Hydraulic pressure pump. On a logging truck, with its own crane for loading, this is an important source of fuel consumption.

## Procedure

Two DV4:s were installed in logging trucks, one in the southern part of Sweden, and one in the north. The weather, the quality of the roads and traffic density differ rather much between these regions. The southern truck was operated by four drivers, the other by two. The drivers were measured for one month. Thereafter, the drivers were trained in using the feedback system, personal handheld computers issued, and the long-term feedback started.

The data was gathered as described above, basically whenever the engine was running, and packaged as units from starting to turning off the engine. However, these continuous runnings were broken down into shorter sections of road by a GPS system. Whenever the vehicle passed a pre-decided location (called a node), a new trip (data package) would be started. This technology had been developed for a previous project concerning the influence of road conditions on fuel consumption. The distances between nodes differed very much, especially between vehicles, as there were fewer nodes in the northern area. This had the effect of introducing a lot of variance between trips.

The data used in the present study was gathered May to August 2003, after feedback had been instigated.

## Variables

A large amount of information was gathered from the engine computer and sensors in the vehicle, and some of it was recomputed for the use as feedback variables to the drivers. The variables used in the present study were mainly the fuel wasting variables a) through d) described above (including fuel used for PTO), shutoff distance and total amount of fuel, but also, distance, total time and time for PTO, braking and idling, all per trip.

## Analyses

Basic descriptive analyses including percentages for each waste factor of total fuel were computed, and thereafter Pearson correlations. After that, forward stepwise multiple regressions were run for each driver's data separately, and then for all combined. Apart from the a) to d) factors, PTO fuel was included as predictor. Beta coefficients and explained variance, partial correlations and B coefficients were calculated.

Furthermore, factor analysis was used to test whether the waste behaviors could be the common result of a higher order faculty, for example a cognitive function.

## RESULTS

It can be seen in tables 1 and 2 that the standard deviations were all very large for behavior variables. This could be expected, as the process for defining a trip make them sample different behaviors at different times, and in absolute values. For example, one trip may be very short in terms of distance and contain mainly PTO and idling. Therefore, most of the distributions were strongly positively skewed.

The time variables in table 2 show that a rather high percentage of the total was PTO-time. This is probably a reflection of the relatively short distances between pickup and offload sites in the south; the two drivers in the north had about 13 percent PTO-time.

**Table 1. The means and standard deviations of the variables used in the regressions. Fuel shown in liters per trip. N=15 466**

| Variable | Total fuel | Idle fuel | PTO fuel | Speed fuel | Gear work fuel | Brake fuel |
|---|---|---|---|---|---|---|
| Mean | 3.673 | 0.067 | 0.284 | 0.047 | 0.113 | 0.194 |
| Std | 10.453 | 0.325 | 1.167 | 0.187 | 0.409 | 0.540 |
| Percent of total fuel | 100.00 | 1.82 | 7.74 | 1.29 | 3.07 | 5.27 |

**Table 2. The means and standard deviations of the time and distance variables. Time shown in seconds, distance in meters, per trip. N=15 466**

| Variable | Total time | Idle time | PTO time | Brake time | Shutoff distance | Distance |
|---|---|---|---|---|---|---|
| Mean | 445.52 | 36.33 | 90.74 | 16.00 | 969.91 | 5628.57 |
| Std | 1145.17 | 152.04 | 387.04 | 40.85 | 3259.22 | 18197.52 |
| Percent of total time | 100 | 8.15 | 20.37 | 3.59 | | |

**Table 3. The Pearson correlations between total fuel, distance and various consumption factors. N=15 466. * p<.001**

| Variable | Idle fuel | PTO fuel | Shutoff distance | Speed fuel | Gear work fuel | Brake fuel | Distance |
|---|---|---|---|---|---|---|---|
| PTO fuel | .44 * | - | | | | | |
| Shutoff distance | .18 * | .05 * | - | | | | |
| Speed fuel | .01 | .00 | .35 * | - | | | |
| Gear work fuel | .26 * | .17 * | .52 * | .18 * | - | | |
| Brake fuel | .19 * | .08 * | .68 * | .36 * | .69 * | - | |
| Distance | .21 * | .06 * | .88 * | .58 * | .51 * | .70 * | - |
| Total fuel | .29 * | .19 * | .89 * | .55 * | .56 * | .73 * | .98 * |

It can be seen in table 3 that the predictor variables tend to be intercorrelated, which of course was expected to some degree, as none of them can really be avoided in the type of work under scrutiny.

In the normal use of multiple regression, the beta weights[3] would be of prime interest. In the present study, however, all variables use the same unit, and the B coefficient may therefore be used for comparisons between variables. As can be seen in tables 4-10 (Drivers 1-4 drove the southern truck), the ranking between variables would seem to be very different using these two, while the semipartial correlations are similar to the beta weights in order of strength.

**Table 4. The regression results for Driver 1; the variance (in percent) of total fuel explained, the beta-weight for each predictor, the semipartial correlation and B coefficient, in order of explanatory strength. Total variance explained 74.37 percent. N=3128**

|                | Variance explained | Beta  | Semipartial correlation | B coefficient |
|----------------|--------------------|-------|-------------------------|---------------|
| Speed fuel     | 53.02              | 0.694 | 0.67                    | 18.83         |
| Brake fuel     | 9.95               | 0.241 | 0.20                    | 2.97          |
| PTO fuel       | 9.40               | 0.292 | 0.29                    | 0.94          |
| Gear work fuel | 1.90               | 0.154 | 0.13                    | 3.77          |
| Idle fuel      | 0.15               | 0.040 | 0.04                    | 1.50          |

**Table 5. The regression results for Driver 2; the variance (in percent) of total fuel explained, the beta-weight for each predictor, the semipartial correlation and B coefficient, in order of explanatory strength. Total variance explained 88.11 percent. N=3731**

|                | Variance explained | Beta   | Semipartial correlation | B coefficient |
|----------------|--------------------|--------|-------------------------|---------------|
| Speed fuel     | 74.84              | 0.703  | 0.62                    | 23.82         |
| Gear work fuel | 10.45              | 0.190  | 0.12                    | 14.22         |
| Brake fuel     | 1.73               | 0.206  | 0.13                    | 4.00          |
| PTO fuel       | 1.08               | 0.113  | 0.11                    | 0.94          |
| Idle fuel      | 0.04               | -0.025 | -0.02                   | -1.89         |

**Table 6. The regression results for Driver 3; the variance (in percent) of total fuel explained, the beta-weight for each predictor, the semipartial correlation and B coefficient, in order of explanatory strength. Total variance explained 82.48 percent. N=3988. The values for Idle fuel were not significant at p<.05**

|                | Variance explained | Beta   | Semipartial correlation | B coefficient |
|----------------|--------------------|--------|-------------------------|---------------|
| Speed fuel     | 62.83              | 0.630  | 0.56                    | 25.25         |
| Brake fuel     | 13.50              | 0.258  | 0.16                    | 3.32          |
| Gear work fuel | 2.23               | 0.191  | 0.12                    | 9.62          |
| PTO fuel       | 1.43               | 0.123  | 0.12                    | 0.82          |
| Idle fuel      | 0.01               | -0.08  | -0.01                   | -0.49         |

---

[3] Normalized measures of impact.

**Table 7. The regression results for Driver 4; the variance (in percent) of total fuel explained, the beta-weight for each predictor, the semipartial correlation and B coefficient, in order of explanatory strength. Total variance explained 82.50 percent. N=3238. The values for Idle fuel were not significant at p<.05**

|  | Variance explained | Beta | Semipartial correlation | B coefficient |
|---|---|---|---|---|
| Brake fuel | 55.22 | 0.395 | 0.24 | 4.80 |
| Speed fuel | 22.45 | 0.531 | 0.49 | 19.82 |
| PTO fuel | 3.46 | 0.157 | 0.15 | 0.88 |
| Gear work fuel | 1.39 | 0.191 | 0.12 | 2.29 |
| Idle fuel | 0.01 | -0.013 | -0.01 | -0.59 |

**Table 8. The regression results for Driver 5; the variance (in percent) of total fuel explained, the beta-weight for each predictor, the semipartial correlation and B coefficient, in order of explanatory strength. Total variance explained 83.16 percent. N=734. PTO fuel was removed from the regression. The values for Gear work fuel were not significant at p<.05**

|  | Variance explained | Beta | Semipartial correlation | B coefficient |
|---|---|---|---|---|
| Brake fuel | 76.36 | 0.707 | 0.31 | 15.87 |
| Speed fuel | 6.40 | 0.280 | 0.25 | 32.83 |
| Idle fuel | 0.46 | 0.062 | 0.06 | 1.84 |
| Gear work fuel | 0.03 | 0.038 | 0.02 | 0.86 |

**Table 9. The regression results for Driver 6; the variance (in percent) of total fuel explained, the beta-weight for each predictor, the semipartial correlation and B coefficient, in order of explanatory strength. Total variance explained 83.77 percent. N=646. The values for Idle fuel were not significant at p<.05**

|  | Variance explained | Beta | Semipartial correlation | B coefficient |
|---|---|---|---|---|
| Brake fuel | 78.39 | 0.623 | 0.37 | 21.80 |
| Speed fuel | 2.65 | 0.191 | 0.16 | 632.319 |
| Gear work fuel | 2.17 | 0.205 | 0.13 | 19.78 |
| PTO fuel | 0.65 | 0.058 | 0.04 | 0.85 |
| Idle fuel | 0.04 | 0.032 | 0.02 | 0.83 |

**Table 10. The results of the multiple regression for the total sample of drivers' trips; the variance (in percent) of total fuel explained, the beta-weight for each predictor, the semipartial correlation and B coefficient, in order of explanatory strength. Total variance explained 66.33 percent. N=15 466**

| Variable | Variance explained | Beta | Semipartial correlation | B coefficient |
|---|---|---|---|---|
| Brake fuel | 52.60 | 0.485 | 0.33 | 9.39 |
| Speed fuel | 9.27 | 0.348 | 0.32 | 19.44 |
| Idle fuel | 3.16 | 0.133 | 0.12 | 4.27 |
| Gear work fuel | 0.86 | 0.121 | 0.09 | 3.09 |
| PTO fuel | 0.45 | 0.075 | 0.07 | 0.67 |

The fuel wasting variables were also studied using factor analysis, but yielded no clear pattern of results. This indicates that the various behaviors measured here are fairly independent from each other, i.e. they do not form a syndrome of interrelated behaviors, despite being somewhat correlated. Neither did separate analyses for each driver yield very interesting results, i.e. no clear factors encompassing all the variables came forward for any driver.

## CONCLUSION

In the present work, one of the aims was to try to estimate how much variance was left unaccounted for, i.e. if other variables that were not included could be of importance. There are, in fact, several variables of interest for the prediction of fuel consumption that have not been used in the present analyses; weather differences, loaded weight, and maybe especially the quality of the roads. This last factor may be a peculiar problem to logging trucks; the roads they use differ very much as to their condition. Given this situation, it is somewhat surprising that such a high degree of variance could be accounted for. This high degree would seem to indicate that the apparatus used does indeed capture a large part of fuel consumption factors, and this to an even higher degree if only driver behavior is considered.

The ranking of the fuel waste factors as to their relative importance would seem to pose an imposing problem; as expected, the answer is guided by the definition of importance. However, it would also seem to be necessary to define for whom, as the drivers show some differences between themselves in their behavior. This, of course, would be expected by a psychologist or driver trainer, but might not always be so self-evident to vehicle manufacturers and other technicians, as driver fuel feedback instruments, for example, seem to be suited to the needs of the vehicle more than to those of the driver.

However, the analyses used here (of the total sample) point in many directions, depending on the many different techniques and coefficients used. Interpreting them one by one, the raw percentages presented first show how much of the overall total that is wasted by the various behaviors measured. Thereafter, the correlations give an inkling what the predictive strength of each behavior is. However, the semipartial correlations show that when all other independent variables are held constant, the predictive power shrinks strongly, i.e. the predictor variables are indeed strongly intercorrelated. However, the relative strength would seem to remain pretty much the same, with the exception of gear work.

The regressions run for the total indicate, by the way of the beta weights and B coefficients, that brake and speed behavior use up a lot of fuel, but as shown by the percentages, they must be relatively uncommon, while using the wrong gear (sub-optimal rpm for the workload) must be very common, as the total effect of this behavior is rather small.

Here the difference between the use of means and percentages, on one hand, and variance-based statistical techniques becomes apparent. Running both types of analyses on a driver's behavior would seem to supplement each other and give a richer picture of what is going on, as well as point out possible ways of attacking problems.

The present study has used as unit of analysis absolute amounts of fuel for each trip undertaken (where trip was defined by engine on/off and geographical locations). It could be argued that the relative amount (liters/km) should have been more appropriate. However, this was certainly not so for the present data; such a treatment further aggravated the outlier problem to absurd levels, causing some scatter plots to become two lines at a ninety degree angle.

The present paper should be viewed as a pilot study on the treatment of fuel consumption variables as measures of driver behavior. As such, it points out several problems in the use of this type of data; mainly the intercorrelations between variables, which create difficulties when using standard psychological statistical methods, but also the conceptual problems in the interpretation of various analyses. It would therefore seem to be the case that traffic psychologists will have to develop new methods, or carefully adapt old ones, to suit the somewhat different needs of fuel-efficient driving studies.

One important lesson to learn from the present data is that when working with real-world behavior measurements, without controls on a number of factors, the resulting analysis will be very sensitive to outliers if correlation measures are used. Unfortunately, outliers would seem to be the rule in this type of data, and it is thus of importance to either set up the method as to rule out these, or else forsake the use of association measures. When interpreting the present results, it should therefore be remembered that the association values are to some part the results of the large ranges of the distributions; if the most extreme values are discarded, the correlations start to shrink. Given the somewhat artificial nature of the range of values (as they are to a large degree due to the very different lengths of the trips), this might be called for. This observation also has some bearing on the problem of non-normal distributions; this was very much an outlier problem.

One limit of the present study is the very small number of drivers involved. Despite the massive amount of data for each of these, it is not possible to draw conclusions about the population of logging truck drivers. There is also the problem of circularity in the data process; are the associations spurious because all data has been calculated using the same software and hardware? This is probably not so, as it was not designed to produce behavior data for the type of analysis done here. However, replications is of course needed, especially given the small number of drivers involved, and the high percentage variation explained.

The adding together of trips undertaken by different drivers would also seem to be a method with some drawbacks; the results do, to some degree, differ. This is especially apparent for idling; although each individual driver would seem to waste very little fuel this way, in terms of variation, the total set of data tells a very different story. This again may be an effect of the very different length of trips, and not really a problem of the method of adding as such, but caution is nevertheless recommended.

Despite these limits, however, the present study does point to some major research questions about the interaction of vehicle technology and driver behavior, and hints to some possible answers. It would seem necessary to do more studies involving the sophisticated hard- and software of electronic measurement technique guided by psychological methodology to achieve results with a bearing on problems in reducing fuel consumption by training and feedback.

# REFERENCES

van de Burgwal, H. C., & Gense, N. L. (2002). *Interpretation of driving style tips.* TNO Report 02.OR.VM.004.1/HVDB. The Netherlands: TNO Automotive.

Govaerts, L., & Verlaak, J. (2003). Eco-Driving in a company fleet. *Mol: Flemish Institute of Technological Research.*

Laurell, H. (1985). *Körsättets betydelse för bränsleförbrukningen.* VTI-rapport 298. Linköping. [*The influence of driving style on fuel consumption.* VTI-report 298].

Nader, J. (1991). Measurement of the impact of driving technique on fuel consumption: Preliminary results. *Roads & Transportation, Technical Note TN-172,* 1-6.

Rothstein, R. N. (1980). Television feedback used to modify gasoline consumption. *Behavior Therapy, 11,* 683-688.

Runnion, A., Watson, J. D., & McWorther, J. (1978). Energy savings in interstate transportation through feedback. *Journal of Organizational Behaviour Management, 1,* 180-191.

Siero, S., Boon, M., Kok, G., & Siero, F. (1989). Modification of driving behaviour in a large transport organization: A field experiment. *Journal of Applied Psychology, 74,* 417-423.

van der Voort, M., Dougherty, M. S., & van Maarseveen, M. (2001). A prototype fuel-efficiency support tool. *Transport Research Part C, 9,* 279-296.

Wouters, P. I., & Bos, J. M. (2000). Traffic accident reduction by monitoring driver behaviour with in-car data recorders. *Accident Analysis and Prevention, 32,* 643-650.

af Wåhlberg, A. E. (2002). Fuel efficient driving training - state of the art and quantification of effects. E141 Proceedings of Soric'02. Available at www.psyk.uu.se/hemsidor/busdriver

af Wåhlberg, A. E. (2006). Short-term effects of training in economical driving; passenger comfort and driver acceleration behavior. *International Journal of Industrial Ergonomics, 36,* 151-163.

af Wåhlberg, A. E. (in press). Long term effects of training in economical driving; fuel consumption, accidents, driver acceleration behavior and technical feedback. *International Journal of Industrial Ergonomics.*

# APPENDIX

## Technical Specification of DV4

- 14,7 MHz 32 bit Processor (ARM-7)
- 4 MB Flash memory
- 2 MB RAM
- 2 Serial ports (rs-232)
- J1708 serial port (RS-485)
- Real time clock
- GSM / GPRS modem
- 1 CAN bus interface (J1939)

## PDA

- Palm Zire 71

The main computer (DV4) is connected to the vehicle ground, battery power, ignition power and J1708 data link layer. Some parts of the DV4, i.e. modem and processor, are powered from the vehicle battery power to ensure that the DV4 is accessible via GSM/GPRS although the vehicle is not actually running. This makes it possible to reprogram and retrieve trips as soon as the DV4 has access to the GSM network.

## Data Input

The data for the calculation of the various variables used in the regression analysis are gathered from various sources. Of main importance for the present study is the independence of total fuel from the other data. Thus, fuel consumption data come from the injection time of the engine, speed from the powertrain, and rpm from the flywheel. Furthermore, the speed fuel variable is calculated from the difference in air resistance of the actual speed as compared to 80 km/h. Brake fuel does also make use of the speed data in conjunction with a sensor on the brake pedal, and the loss is calculated from the difference in velocity during the time the pedal is depressed.

PTO, gear work and idle are simpler; these register the amount of fuel used when the hydraulic system is engaged, the clutch depressed and speed zero, respectively.

## System Architecture

The System architecture is divided in four layers of data processing;

- Physical
- Pre-processing
- Main data processing
- Back-office processing

### Physical Layer

The main function is to collect raw data from the vehicle internal data bus, such as vehicle speed, engine speed, engine load, fuel rate, clutch- and brake pedal engagement. Each parameter is converted to SI-units and transported to the next layer.

### Pre-Processing Layer

Incorrect, inaccurate or missing data needed for the main data processing which is calculated from parameter sets specific for each vehicle configuration. Torque, power and fuel rate is some of the most frequently modified or calculated parameters due to simplified parameter definitions from the vehicle manufacturer. This layer guarantees that sufficient amount of data is transported to the next layer.

### Main Data Processing Layer

This layer mainly has three tasks;

Generate basic statistics.
Generate behavior statistics.
Generate feedback to driver via PDA.

## Basic Statistics

Generates statistics based on the basic data delivered by the pre-processing layer. These data spans from simple variables such as distance to more complex dependent products of the basic data such as engine efficiency.

## Behavior Statistics

To calculate behavior-related statistics, the system first have to recognize a pattern of data, determine start and stop of the behavior and then finally calculate the effects of it. The accumulated behavior-related data is stored together with the basic statistics in the trip.

There are mainly five fuel-wasting behaviors taken into account, see definitions below.

- Brake
- Idle
- Gear
- High velocity
- Gear work

### Brake

When braking the driver converts energy, previously invested in vehicle velocity, into heat. The corresponding fuel-waste depends on the retardation undertaken, velocity and mass.

### Idle

When the driver does not turn off the engine even though the vehicle is not moving and PTO is not active.

### Gear

Loss due to not driving the vehicle in the most fuel-efficient gear (sub optimal rpm). Note that this variable was not included in the present study, due to technical difficulties.

### High Velocity

The extra energy the engine has to produce to overcome 80 km/h. The air resistance is strongly determined by the velocity.

### Gear Work

The amount of fuel consumed during change of gear.

Measured is also the opposite of braking; shut-off distance, meaning the time spent in engine braking.

## Feedback to the Driver via PDA

The PDA gives the driver information about the momentary fuel economy and a 30 second history of his fuel consumption (histogram). The histogram is intended to assist the driver to drive fuel efficiently in his everyday work.

## Back-Office Processing

As soon as trips are downloaded from the vehicle into the server database, the data has to be presented and merged in such a way that the information becomes useful for both driver and company. This data can be merged in numerous ways for the end user via a web interface distributed through VDI Innovation.

In: Industrial Psychology Research Trends
Editor: Ina M. Pearle, pp. 89-103

ISBN: 978-1-60021-825-5
© 2007 Nova Science Publishers, Inc.

Chapter 5

# THE ROLE OF PSYCHOSOCIAL WORK ENVIRONMENT IN PSYCHOLOGICAL HEALTH AND WELL-BEING AMONG HEALTH CARE STAFF

*Bettina F. Piko and Martha Piczil*
University of Szeged, Hungary

## ABSTRACT

It is well known that job stress influences employees' work satisfaction, physical and mental health and well-being. The present paper includes results of two independent studies. First, we have analyzed the potential influencing characteristics of work environment related to nurses' life satisfaction with special emphasis put on burnout factors. Second, the next study has been to look at the relationship between psychosocial work environment and self-perceived health in a sample of health care staff living and working in Subotica, Serbia. In the first study, there were 201 registered nurses working in Szeged hospitals, Hungary. In the second study, there were 253 health care workers in the sample, most of them worked as registered nurses, head nurses or assistants (altogether 80.1% of them). The data collection was going on by means of self-administered questionnaires. The health care staff as respondents report a high frequency of experiencing emotionally provoking situations. Parallel with this, they often lack the social network which would provide effective support in these situations. The frequencies of emotionally provoking situations and the lack of social support, together with the paid extra work and the low levels of work satisfaction influence negatively their self-perceived health. Findings also suggest that burnout factors are significantly related to life satisfaction, the relationship is particularly strong with emotional exhaustion. Work satisfaction shows a strong relationship with the three burnout subscales, in addition, the relationship between life satisfaction and work satisfaction is particularly strong. These results draw the attention to the role of psychosocial work environment in determining satisfaction with life as an indicator of subjective well-being. In addition, the psychosocial work environment significantly has an impact on the health care workers' self-perceived health and their levels of psychosomatic symptoms. There is a great need of learning skills and techniques among health care staff which would help them in preventing deterioration of their psychological health and well-being.

**Keywords:** psychosocial work environment; satisfaction with life; work satisfaction; psychological health and well-being.

# INTRODUCTION

Job stress is a process in which some characteristics of the work or workplace have harmful consequence for employees (Beehr and Franz, 1985). The literature suggests that there are three major sources of stressors in the workplace, namely, the task and its characteristics; interpersonal relationships; and the features of the organization (Beehr, 1991). Work stress is a part of the psychosocial environment of the workplace (Flarey, 1991). Stressful psychosocial work environment has serious impact on employees' health and well-being including many physiological, psychological, behavioral and social consequences (Lambert, Lambert, and Ito, 2004; Leiter, 1992). The individuals experience a number of strains, such as insomnia, psychosomatic symptoms, anxiety or depression (Eels, Lacefield, and Maxey, 1994). The organization experience a number of negative features, such as low level of work satisfaction, high labor turnover and burnout symptoms among the employees (Murray, 2002).

The issue of job-related stress among health care staff is particularly a major concern throughout the world (Wheeler and Riding, 1994). Health professionals are exposed to a great number of stressors day by day (Gelsema et al., 2006). Besides the physical stressors, psychological stressors are closely connected with their job, such as the high degree of responsibility, interpersonal conflicts with peers, supervisors and patients, the irregular work schedule, the pressure of workload, the great number of emotionally provoking situations (Escriba-Agüir and Tenias-Burillo, 2004; Piko, 2003; Zammuner and Galli, 2005). Within the health service, nursing is invariably assumed to be a stressful professional field (Piko, 1999). Job-related stress may be particularly hazardous when nurses lack the appropriate social support from their colleagues or when they do not possess effective coping skills (Fenlason and Beehr, 1994; Lambert, Lambert, and Ito, 2004).

Nursing belongs to helping professionals who are at special high risk for deterioration of somatic and psychosocial health (Piko, 1999). The high level of physical and psychological workload may often lead to burnout syndrome which implies the following: depersonalization; a lower level of accomplishment; and emotional exhaustion (Maslach and Goldberg, 1998; Spickard Jr., Gabbe, and Christensen, 2002). Due to burnout syndrome, nurses intention to leave increases, their self-image and health deteriorates (Jeanneau and Armelius, 2000; Leiter, 1992; Murray, 2002; Ramirez et al., 1996). There is a close connection between burnout and work satisfaction (Faragher, Cass, and Cooper, 2005; Kalliath and Morris, 2002). In addition, there are strong intercorrelations among burnout, role conflict, job satisfaction, and psychosomatic health among nurses (Piko, 2006a).

Since health is a complex concept, there is a need for using multiple health indicators in surveys. Among the health indicators, self-perceived health is an appropriate psychosocial health indicator which reflects both the objective health status (Heistaro et al., 2001), and the subjective experiences (Goodwin and Engstrom, 2002). Based on many population studies, the reliability of such self-assessments has been found to be good (Lundberg and Manderbacka, 1996). As a global health evaluation, self-perceived health is widely used measuring health in studies. Global self-evaluations, such as self-perceived health, do not focus on a specific dimension of health but provide a succinct way of summarizing the diverse components of health (Ware Jr., 1986). The psychosocial dimension of health tends to play an increasing role in determining health, illness and quality of life in modern society (Macleod and Davey Smith, 2005).

Not surprisingly, psychosocial work environment may have a great impact on self-perceived health and the development of psychosomatic symptoms and other stress-related illness (Krantz and Oestergren, 2000; Lennon, 1994). In addition, nurses' psychosocial work environment influences their levels of job satisfaction and their intention to keep or leave their career (Tumulty, Jernigan, and Kohut, 1994; Yoder, 1995). We should also note here that female health care workers usually have a double workload stemming from household duties or extra paid work due to low salaries (Ross and Bird, 1994; Walters et al., 1997). Job satisfaction seems to be a good indicator of the psychosocial work environment and the stress-related health problems (Lu, While, and , Barriball, 2004).

Among the indicators of psychosocial health and well-being, satisfaction with life is considered to be a key issue in the field of measuring the quality of life (Ryan and Deci, 2001). Satisfaction with life, as a global indicator, is an element of subjective well-being (Diener et al., 1999). Among the indicators of general satisfaction, there are specific indicators, such as the satisfaction with life, health, work, etc. Work satisfaction, that is, satisfaction with work environment, or work conditions, is closely connected with the level of satisfaction with life (Büssing et al., 1999; Lee et al., 2004; Mackenzie, Poulin, and Seidman-Carlson, 2006). Whereas high level of work satisfaction may elevate our life spirits and help develop an optimistic attitude toward life, low level of work satisfaction may contribute to many life problems. Furthermore, low satisfaction with life is a serious health risk factor since it may contribute to deterioration of mental and physical health and elevate the risk of early mortality (Koivumaa-Honkanen et al., 2000). Among nurses, burnout has been found to be a key factor contributing to low level of work satisfaction (Faragher, Cass, and Cooper, 2005). The connection between burnout and life satisfaction, however, is a less investigated field of research. In a recent study, Lee and coworkers (2004) have found that burnout experiences influence the level of satisfaction with life, more than the level of work satisfaction. Among the elemenst of burnout syndrome, decrease of personal accomplishment and emotional exhaustion are the most important ones influencing life satisfaction, whereas depersonalization shows less influence.

The main goal of the present study is two-fold. First, we aim at investigating the role of psychosocial work environment in levels of satisfaction with life among health care staff. Second, we also aim at analyzing the role of psychosocial work environment in nurses' self-perceived health. We have used two independent data-sets to analyze these relationships in multivariate models.

# STUDY 1

## Subjects and Method

Respondents for this study were selected from two major hospitals in Szeged, Hungary. Besides university hospitals, these two sites provide health care for people in and around Szeged. Anonymous questionnaires were distributed to 450 health care staff (the total number of health care staff working in various hospital units), among whom 55.7% were registered nurses, the others has various paramedical jobs like assistants, physician's or nurse's aides. The questionnaires were delivered to and collected in staff meetings in all hospital units by trained sociology students over a 4-week period. Response rate from the two organizations was 44.6%. This was lower than expected but could be explained by low motivation of health care staff stemming from uncertainty and psychosocial stress due to the ongoing health care reform. All together, 201 questionnaires were returned and analyzed.

Self-completed questionnaires were used to collect data on work and health-related information, besides some basic sociodemographics.

*Satisfaction with life* was measured by The Satisfaction With Life Scale (Diener et al., 1985). This measurement is a widely used scale in Hungarian populations (Piko, 2006b). The scale consisted of five statements, such as "In most ways my life is close to ideal." The participants indicated how strongly they agreed with each item from 1 ("strongly disagree") to 7 ("strongly agree"). The final scale had a range of 5-35 with a Cronbach's alpha value of 0.87.

*Burnout* was measured using the Maslach Burnout Inventory (MBI; Maslach and Jackson, 1981), which has been also widely used in Hungarian studies (e.g., Piko, 2006a). This is a 22-item measure containing three subscales, namely, emotional exhaustion, depersonalization, and personal accomplishment. More burnout is indicated higher scores on emotional exhaustion and depersonalization, and lower scores on personal accomplishment. Internal consistency was measured using Cronbach's alpha with reliability coefficients of 0.84 for emotional exhaustion, 0.46 for depersonalization and 0.76 for personal accomplishment with the present sample. All these values are consistent with a previous study from Norway (Richardsen, Burke, and Leiter, 1992), in which Cronbach's alpha for depersonalization was the lowest (0.51) and that for emotional exhaustion was the highest (0.84).

*Job satisfaction* was measured by four items (Beehr, King, and King, 1990). Each of the four items measured global assessment of the job rather than judgements of specific aspects (e.g., "All in all, how satisfied would you say you are with your job?" or "If a friend of yours told you he /she was interested in working in a job like yours what would you tell him/her?") The scores were summed and thus the final scale has a range of 4-12 and was reliable with a Cronbach's alpha of 0.74. In addition, the perceived level of health care staff's *social prestige* (7-point scale) and *the number of years spent in health care* were also asked.

SPSS for MS Windows Release 11.0 program was used in the calculations with a maximum significance level set at .05. The analyses begin with a descriptive statistics for the variables. Besides, correlation analysis was applied to determine bivariate relationships. Finally, multiple regression estimates were calculated to present the role of burnout factors and other work-related variables in influencing satisfaction with life among health care staff.

## Results

Table 1 presents the descriptive statistics for study variables, such as sociodemographics, the elements of burnout syndrome, other work-related factors, and the level of satisfaction with life among health care staff in this sample.

**Table 1. Descriptive statistics for study variables (N = 201)**

|  | % | Mean (S.D.) |
|---|---|---|
| Sociodemographics |  |  |
| Age (years) (min.: 20, max.: 64) |  | 33.1 (14.1) |
| Gender |  |  |
| Males | 11.1 |  |
| Females | 88.9 |  |
| Schooling |  |  |
| Primary school | 5.1 |  |
| Apprenticeship | 16.7 |  |
| Secondary vocational school | 45.5 |  |
| Secondary modern school (high school) | 23.7 |  |
| College degree | 9.1 |  |
|  |  |  |
| Work-related variables |  |  |
| Years spent in health care |  | 14.9 (10.8) |
| Satisfaction with work (score: 4-12) |  | 8.2 (1.9) |
| Perceived level of social prestige (score: 1-7) |  | 2.9 (1.8) |
|  |  |  |
| Burnout syndrome |  |  |
| Emotional exhaustion (score: 10-39) |  | 24.7 (6.2) |
| Depersonalization (score: 5-21) |  | 9.4 (3.3) |
| Personal accomplishment (score: 14-40) |  | 27.4 (4.4) |
|  |  |  |
| Satisfaction with life (score: 0-27) |  | 10.3 (6.4) |

There were 11.1% males and 88.9% females in the sample. Due to the small sample size, we do not apply gender as an influencing variables in further analyses. Regarding educational level, most of the respondents (45.5%) report secondary vocational school background. The mean age of the sample was 33.1 years, whereas the number of years spent in health care was 15 years. The perceived level of social prestige was rather low, the level of job satisfaction was medium-size. The level of life satisfaction does not reach the 50% of the total point.

Table 2 shows a correlational matrix for work-related variables.

**Table 2. Correlation matrix for work-related variables**

| | Satisfaction with life | Work satisfaction | Schoolin g | Social prestige | Emotional exhaustion | Depersonalization |
|---|---|---|---|---|---|---|
| Satisfaction with life | - | - | - | - | - | - |
| Work satisfaction | 0.32*** | - | - | - | - | - |
| Schooling | 0.22** | -0.07 | - | - | - | - |
| Social prestige | 0.21** | 0.08 | 0.01 | - | - | - |
| Emotional exhaustion | -0.35*** | -0.53*** | -0.06 | -0.11 | - | - |
| Depersonalization | 0.15* | -0.41*** | -0.08 | -0.03 | 0.59*** | - |
| Personal accomplishment | 0.32*** | 0.43*** | 0.08 | 0.04 | -0.45*** | -0.37*** |

*p<.05; **p<.01  ***p<.001.

Life satisfaction positively correlated with work satisfaction. Among the burnout variables, personal accomplishment positively, whereas emotional exhaustion and depersonalization negatively correlated with work satisfaction. Similar relationships could be detected in relation to life satisfaction, except for depersonalization which correlated positively with the satisfaction with life.

Finally, table 3 presents multiple regression estimates for the satisfaction with life variable. In the first column, the effects of burnout syndrome are displayed. Emotional exhaustion was a negative, whereas personal accomplishment was a positive predictor of life satisfaction. Among other work-related variables (second column), work satisfaction, schooling, years spent in health care and perceived social prestige also significantly and positively related to life satisfaction. In the final model, emotional exhaustion (as negative predictor), work satisfaction and schooling (as positive predictors) remain significant. All these variables explained 24% of variation in the dependent variable.

**Table 3. Multiple regression estimates for the satisfaction with life (N=201)**

| Independent variables | Satisfaction with life | | |
|---|---|---|---|
| | Model 1 | Model 2 | Model 3 |
| Burnout syndrome | | | |
| Emotional exhaustion | -0.31***[a] | | -0.22* |
| Depersonalization | 0.09 | | 0.09 |
| Personal accomplishment | 0.22** | | 0.11 |
| Other work-related variables | | | |
| Work satisfaction | | 0.32*** | 0.20* |
| Schooling | | 0.23** | 0.21** |
| Years spent in health care | | 0.13* | 0.13 |
| Perceived social prestige | | 0.17* | 0.14 |
| Constant | 7.992 | -2.338 | 0.00 |
| $R^2$ | 0.17*** | 0.20*** | 0.24*** |

*p<.05; ;**p<.01;***p<.001.
Note. aStandardized regression coefficients.

# STUDY 2

## Subjects and Method

Respondents for this study were selected from the Primary Health Care Service in Subotica, Serbia (approx. 50 miles from the Hungarian-Serbian border with joint historical roots). All together, 253 health care staff participated in the study. Among the respondents, 33.2% completed Hungarian, whereas 66.8% of them completed Serbian language questionnaires. In the sample, there were 90.5% females. The mean age of the respondents was 29 years of age, the avegare age (years) spent in health care was 10 years. Regarding their employment status, 12.8% of them worked as a nurse, 12.2% as a head nurse, 55.1% as an assistant, 0.5% as a physician's aide, 0.5% as a nurse' aide, and 18.9% of them as other paramedical staff. Respondents participating in the study had three main types of work schedule: permanent morning (60.1%), rotating day (28.4%) and rotating night (11.0%), only

0.5% of them reported working in permanent night shift (therefore, we skipped them in further analyses) (table 1).

A self-completed questionnaire was used as a method of data collection which included items on sociodemographics, self-perceived health as well as other health and work-related variables.

*Self-perceived health* as a global health indicator was measured by asking respondents how they compared their health status to their peers. The responses included: poor = 1; fair = 2; good = 3; and excellent = 4 (Piko, 1999).

*Psychosomatic symptom* scale included the following self-reported symptoms: lower-back pain, tension headache, sleeping problems, chronic fatigue, stomach pyrosis, tension diarrhea and heart palpitation. This measure was used in order to obtain information on the frequency of these symptoms during the last 12 months (Piko, Barabas, and Boda, 1997). Respondents were asked: "During the past 12 months, how often have you had a back-pain?"...etc. Responses were coded as often (4), sometimes (3), seldom (2), and never (1). The final scale had a range of 7-28 and was reliable with a Cronbach's alpha of 0.80.

Among the *work-related variables*, the following ones were measured: years spent in health care, work satisfaction, occurrence of emotionally provoking situations, and social support from colleagues in these situations. *Work satisfaction* was measured by four items (Beehr, King, and King, 1990). Each of the four items (e.g., "All in all, how satisfied would you say you are with your job?" or "If a friend of yours told you he /she was interested in working in a job like yours what would you tell him/her?") measured global assessment of the job rather than judgements of specific aspects. The final scale had a range of 4-12 and was reliable with a Cronbach's alpha of 0.82. The occurrence of *emotionally provoking situations* was measured by the following question: "How often do you experience problems at work which are emotionally provoking for you?" Nurses also were asked about *social support* from colleagues: "How often do you receive social support from peers at work when you are in need of it?" Response categories in relation to the previous two measures were: never (1), seldom (2), sometimes (3), and often (4) (Piko, 2003).

SPSS for MS Windows Release 11.0 program was used in the calculations with a maximum significance level set at .05. The analyses begin with a descriptive statistics for the study variables. The bivariate relationships among the variables were determined by correlation analysis. Finally, we calculated odds ratios which helped detect the bivariate relationships between respondents' self-perceived health, and a set of independent variables (health and work-related factors). The self-perceived health variable was dichotomized and expressed wither poor/fair or good/excellent perceptions of one's own health. The main goal of the analysis was to detect differences between those who perceive their own health better and lower with regards to variables reflecting possible risk for fair/poor perceptions. The results of the binary logistic regression analyses are presented as a series of odds. The baseline odds are set to 1.0. An odds ratio > 1.0 indicates that there is a positive association between the factors of interest to the baseline odds while a value < 1.0 indicates the inverse. Confidence intervals (95%) were also calculated for statistically significant relationships based on the criterion that the CIs did not include 1.0

# RESULTS

**Table 1. Descriptive statistics for the study variables (N = 253)**

|  | % | Mean (S.D.) |
|---|---|---|
| Sociodemographics | | |
| Age (years) | | 29.2 (12.9) |
| Ethnicity | | |
| Hungarian | 33.2 | |
| Serbian | 66.8 | |
| Work-related variables | | |
| Years spent in health care | | 10.1 (12.4) |
| Work satisfaction (score: 4-12) | | 9.5 (2.1) |
| Work schedule | | |
| Permanent morning | 60.1 | |
| Rotating day | 28.4 | |
| Rotating night | 11.0 | |
| Permanent night | 0.5 | |
| Emotionally provoking situations | | |
| Often | 32.5 | |
| Sometimes | 42.3 | |
| Seldom | 19.2 | |
| Never | 6.0 | |
| Social support from colleagues | | |
| Often | 17.0 | |
| Sometimes | 34.9 | |
| Seldom | 31.4 | |
| Never | 16.6 | |
| Paid extra work | | |
| No | 65.5 | |
| Yes, job-related | 9.8 | |
| Yes, non job-related | 24.7 | |
| Health-related variables | | |
| Self-perceived health | | |
| Excellent | 20.7 | |
| Good | 49.8 | |
| Fair | 25.9 | |
| Poor | 3.6 | |
| Psychosomatic symptom scale (score: 7-28) | | 17.1 (5.0) |

Table 2. presents a correlation matrix for the study variables. Older health care staff report more emotionally provoking situations and they tend to engage in paid extra work. They also report more psychosomatic symptoms and they are less satisfied with their own health. Emotionally provoking situations variable correlated negatively, whereas social support correlated positively with work satisfaction. There is a positive correlation between work satisfaction and self-perceived health.

**Table 2. Correlation matrix for the work and health-related variables**

| | Years spent in health care | Emotionally provoking situations | Social support | Paid extra work | Work satisfaction | Self-perceived health | Psycho-somatic symptoms |
|---|---|---|---|---|---|---|---|
| Age | 0.99*** | 0.30*** | 0.01 | 0.19** | 0.06 | -0.40*** | 0.13* |
| Years spent in health care | - | 0.31*** | -0.01 | 0.19* | 0.05 | -0.40*** | 0.14* |
| Emotionally provoking situations | - | - | -0.01 | 0.08 | -0.29*** | -0.29*** | 0.35*** |
| Social support | - | - | - | -0.03 | 0.21** | 0.12* | 0.03 |
| Paid extra work | - | - | - | - | -0.06 | -0.16* | 0.01 |
| Work satisfaction | - | - | - | - | - | 0.16** | -0.21** |
| Self-perceived health | - | - | - | - | - | - | -0.39*** |
| Psychosomatic symptoms | - | - | - | - | - | - | - |

*p<.05; **p<.01; ***p<.001.

The results of calculated odds ratios for the relationship between self-perceived health and other variables are shown in table 3. Among sociodemographics, age (OR = 1.2) and the years spent in health care (OR = 1.2) were significant predictors of self-perceived health, whereas ethnicity was not. Rotating night shift (OR = 2.7) and non job-related extra work (OR = 2.2) also were predictors. Frequent psychosomatic symptoms (OR = 1.2) and emotionally provoking situations (OR = 3.9 as often) were also associated with an increased likelihood of poor/fair perceptions of health. Finally, work satisfaction (OR = 0.8) and social support (OR = 0.3 as often) proved to be protective factors.

**Table 3. Estimated Odds Ratios (OR) of the effects of sociodemographics, health and work-related variables on the likelihood of poor/fair self-perceived health**

| Predictor variables | Poor/fair perception of health OR[b] (95% CI)[c] |
|---|---|
| Age | 1.2 (1.1 – 1.9)* |
| Years spent in health care | 1.2 (1.1 – 1.9)** |
| Ethnicity | |
| Hungarian[a] | 1.0 |
| Serbian | 0.8 (0.5 – 1.5) |
| Work schedule | |
| Permanent morning[a] | 1.0 |
| Rotating day | 1.1 (0.4 – 3.1) |
| Rotating night | 2.7 (1.4 – 5.4)** |
| Psychosomatic symptoms | 1.2 (1.1 – 1.4)*** |
| Emotionally provoking situations | |
| Never[a] | 1.0 |
| Seldom | 0.5 (0.3 – 2.2) |
| Sometimes | 1.2 (0.3 – 4.4) |
| Often | 3.9 (1.1 – 14.9)** |
| Social support from colleagues | |
| Never[a] | 1.0 |
| Seldom | 0.7 (0.3 – 1.5) |
| Sometimes | 0.7 (0.3 – 1.6) |
| Often | 0.3 (0.1 – 0.9)* |
| Paid extra work | |
| No[a] | 1.0 |
| Yes, job-related | 0.1 (0.3 – 2.3) |
| Yes, other type | 2.2 (1.1 – 4.2)** |
| Work satisfaction | 0.8 (0.6 – 0.9)* |

[a]Reference categories; [b]OR, Odds Ratio; [c]95% Confidence Intervals.

# DISCUSSION

The main goal of the present study has been to investigate relationships between indicators of psychological health (namely, satisfaction with life and self-perceived health), and a set of work-related variables. Previous studies indicate that psychosocial work environment has a great impact on employees' mental and somatic health, well-being and quality of life (Eels, Lacefield, and Maxey, 1994; Flarey, 1991; Lambert, Lambert, and Ito, 2004; Leiter, 1992; Piko, 2003; Piko, 2006a). Certain health status and well-being measurements may serve as an indicator of job-related stress, such as psychosomatic symptoms, self-perceived health or the level of satisfaction with life (Lee et al., 2004; Lu, While, and , Barriball, 2004; Piko, 1999). Despite these facts, however, very few studies have investigated these interrelationships in Hungary and Serbia thus far. Therefore, these two studies were an initial phase of investigating the role of psychosocial work environment in health and well-being among health care staff in this region.

Working in the health care system is invariably a stressful job (Escriba-Agüir and Tenias-Burillo, 2004; Gelsema et al., 2006; Wheeler and Riding, 1994). Burnout is a central feature of job-related stress (Maslach and Goldberg, 1998; Piko, 2006a). The descriptive data for burnout variables shows that the mean for emotional exhaustion is slightly lower, that of depersonalization is slightly higher, and the mean score for personal accomplishment is much lower than data for health care workers in Norway (Richardsen, Burke, and Leiter, 1992). Comparing to social service workers from Canada, both emotional exhaustion and depersonalization are higher among Hungarian health care staff, whereas personal accomplishment is much lower (Leiter, 1992). In comparison with US nurses, emotional exhaustion is slightly lower, depersonalization is considerably lower, and personal accomplishment is much higher than data from Hungarian health care staff (Oehler et al., 1991; Jorgensen Dick, 1992). According to ranges for low, moderate and high burnout for each subscale as suggested by Maslach and Jackson (1981), the subscales of emotional exhaustion and depersonalization show moderate, scores on personal accomplishment show high levels of experienced burnout. All these mean that this sample of Hungarian health care staff experience relatively high levels of burnout.

In addition, we may also conclude that these high levels of burnout had a significant influence on work satisfaction as well as life satisfaction, similar to previous studies (Faragher, Cass, and Cooper, 2005; Lee et al., 2004). Among the burnout variables, emotional exhaustion was a negative, whereas personal accomplishment was a positive predictor of life satisfaction. Among other work-related variables, work satisfaction, schooling, years spent in health care and perceived social prestige were also significantly and positively related to life satisfaction.

Besides satisfaction with life as a global indicator of well-being, self-perceived health is also a global indicator of health and well-being (Goodwin and Engstrom, 2002; Lundberg and Manderbacka, 1996; Piko, Barabas, and Boda, 1997). Poor self-perceived health has been found to be a good indicator of job-related stress as well (Piko, 1999). Our findings suggest that rotating night shift, non job-related extra work, frequent psychosomatic symptoms and emotionally provoking situations were associated with an increased likelihood of poor/fair perceptions of health. Besides these job-related risk factors, work satisfaction and social support proved to be protective factors. Previous studies also report a positive relationship between work satisfaction and health (Lu, While, and , Barriball, 2004). Furthermore, social support has been found to serve as a protection against harmful health consequences of job-related stress (Fenlason and Beehr, 1994; Piko, 1999; Piko, 2003).

Results of these studies underline the importance of the role of psychosocial work environment in health and well-being among health care staff. Findings suggest that improvement in this field should be a priority intervention during the ongoing socio-economic reforms. Information on psychosocial work environment may provide a good basis for such an intervention.

## REFERENCES

Beehr, T.A. (1991). Stress in the workplace: An overview. In: Jones, J.W., Steffy, B.D., Bray, D.W. (eds.): *Applying psychology in business*. Lexington, MA, Lexington, pp. 58-67.

Beehr, T.A., King, L.A., King, D.W. (1991). Social support and occupational stress: Talking to supervisors. *Journal of Vocational Behavior*, 36, 61-81.

Beehr, T.A., Franz, T.M. (1985). The current debate about the meaning of job stress. *Journal of Occupational Behavior Management*, 8, 5-18.

Büssing, A., Bissels, T., Fuchs, V., Perrar, K.-M. (1999). A dynamic model of work satisfaction: Qualitative approaches. *Human Relations*, 52, 999-1027.

Diener, E., Emmons, R.A., Larsen, R.J., Griffin, S. (1985). The Satisfaction With Life Scale. *Journal of Personality Assessment*, 49, 71-75.

Diener, E., Suh, E.M., Lucas, R.E., Smith, H.L. (1999). Subjective well-being: Three decades of progress. *Psychological Bulletin,* 125, 276-302.

Eels, T., Lacefield, P., Maxey, J. (1994). Symptom correlates and factor structure of the Health Professions Stress Inventory. *Psychological Reports*, 75, 1563-1568.

Escriba-Agüir, V., Tenias-Burillo, J.M. (2004). Psychological well-being among hospital personnel: The role of family demands and psychosocial work environment. *International Archives of Occupational and Environmental Health,* 77, 401-408.

Faragher, E.B., Cass, M., Cooper, C.L. (2005). The relationship between job satisfaction and health: A metaanalysis. *Occupational and Environmental Medicine*, 62, 105-112.

Fenlason, K.J., Beehr, T.A. (1994). Social support and occupational stress: Effects of talking to others. *Journal of Organizational Behavior*, 15, 157-175.

Flarey, D.L. (1991). The social climate scale: A tool for organizational change and development. *Journal of Nursing Administration*, 21, 37-44.

Gelsema, T.I., van der Doef, M., Maes, S., Janssen, M., Akerboom, S., Verhoeven, C. (2006). A longitudinal study of job stress in the nursing profession: Causes and consequences. *Journal of Nursing Management*, 14, 289-299.

Goodwin, R., Engstrom, G. (2002). Personality and the perception of health in the general population. *Psychological Medicine*, 32, 325-332.

Heistaro, S., Jousilahti, P., Lahelma, E., Vartiainen, E., Puska, P. (2001). Self-rated health and mortality: A long term prospective study in eastern Finland. *Journal of Epidemiology and Community Health*, 55, 227-232.

Jeanneau, M., Armelius, K. (2000). Self-image and burnout in psychiatric staff. *Journal of Psychiatric and Mental Health Nursing*, 7, 399-406.

Jorgensen Dick, M. (1992). Burnout in doctorally prepared nurse faculty. *Journal of Nursing Education*, 31, 341-346.

Kalliath, T., Morris, R. (2002). Job satisfaction among nurses: A predictor of burnout levels. *Journal of Nursing Administration*, 32, 648-654.

Koivumaa-Honkanen, H., Honkanen, R., Viinamäki, H., Heikkila, K., Kaprio, J.,Koskenvuo, M. (2000). Self-reported life satisfaction and 20-year mortality in healthy Finnish adults. *American Journal of Epidemiology*, 152, 983-991.

Krantz, G., Östergren, P.-O. (2000). Common symptom in middle aged women: Their relation to employment status, psychosocial work conditions and social support in a Swedish setting. *Journal of Epidemiology and Community Health*, 54, 192-199.

Lambert, V.A., Lambert, C.E., Ito, M. (2004). Workplace stressors, ways of coping and demographic characteristics as predictors of physical and mental health of Japanese hospital nurses. *International Journal of Nursing Studies*, 41, 85-97.

Lee, H., Hwang, S., Kim, J., Daly, B. (2004). Predictors of life satisfaction of Korean nurses. *Journal of Advanced Nursing*, 48, 632-641.

Leiter, M.P. (1992). Burnout as a crisis in professional role structures: Measurement and conceptual issues. *Anxiety, Stress and Coping*, 5, 79-93.

Lennon, M.C. (1994). Women, work, and well-being: The importance of work conditions. *Journal of Health and Social Behavior*, 35, 235-247.

Lu, H., While, A.E., Barriball, K.L. (2004). Job satisfaction among nurses: A review of the literature. *International Journal of Nursing Studies*, 42, 211-227.

Lundberg, O., Manderbacka, K. (1996). Assessing reliability of a measure of self-rated health. *Scandinavian Journal of Social Medicine*, 24, 218-224.

Mackenzie, C.S., Poulin, P.A., Seidman-Carlson, R. (2006). A brief mindfulness-based stress reduction intervention for nurses and nurse aides. *Applied Nursing Research*, 19, 105-109.

Macleod, J., Davey Smith, G. (2005). Psychosocial factors and public health: A suitable case for treatment? *Journal of Epidemiology and Community Health*, 57, 565-570.

Maslach, C., Jackson, S.E. (1981). *Maslach Burnout Inventory*. Consulting Psychologists Press, Palo Alto, CA.

Maslach, C., Goldberg, J. (1998). Prevention of burnout: New perspectives. *Applied and Preventive Psychology*, 7, 63-74.

Murray, M.K. (2002). The nursing shortage: Past, present, and future. *Journal of Nursing Administration*, 32, 79-84.

Oehler, J., Davidson, G.M., Starr, L., Lee, D.A. (1991). Burnout, job stress, anxiety, and perceived social support in neonatal jurses. *Heart and Lung*, 20, 500-505.

Piko, B., Barabas, K., Boda, K. (1997). Frequency of common psychosomatic symptoms and its influence on self-perceived health in a Hungarian student population. *European Journal of Public Health*, 7, 243-247.

Piko, B. (1999). Work-related stress among nurses: A challenge for health care institutions. *Journal of The Royal Society for the Promotion of Health*, 119, 156-162.

Piko, B.F. (2003). Psychosocial work environment and psychosomatic health of nurses in Hungary. *Work and Stress*, 17, 93-100.

Piko, B.F. (2006a). Burnout, role conflict, job satisfaction and psychosocial health among Hungarian health care staff. *International Journal of Nursing Studies*, 43, 311-318.

Piko, B.F (2006b). Satisfaction with life, psychosocial health, and materialism among Hungarian youth. *Journal of Health Psychology*, 11, 827-831.

Ramirez, A.J., Graham, J., Richard, M.A., Cull, A., Gregory, W.M. (1996). Mental health of hospital consultants: The effects of stress and satisfaction at work. *Lancet*, 16, 724-728.

Richardsen, A.M., Burke, R.J., Leiter, M.P. (1992). Occupational demands, psychological burnout and anxiety among hospital personnel in Norways. *Anxiety, Stress and Coping*, 5, 55-68.

Ross, C.E., Bird, C.E. (1994). Sex stratification and health lifestyle: Consequences for men's and women's perceived health. *Journal of Health and Social Behavior*, 35, 161-178.

Ryan, R.M., Deci, E.L. (2001). On happiness and human potentials: A review of research on hedonic and eudaimonic well-being. *Annual Review of Psychology*, 52, 141-166.

Spickard, Jr., A., Gabbe, S.G., Christensen, J.F. (2002). Mid-career burnout in generalist and specialist physicians. *Journal of the American Medical Association*, 288, 1447-1450.

Tumulty, G., Jernigan, I.E., Kohut, G.F. (1994). The impact of perceived work environment on job satisfaction of hospital staff nurses. *Applied Nursing Research*, 7, 84-90.

Walters, V., French, S., Eyles, J., Lenton, R., Newbold, B., Mayr, J. (1997). The effects of paid and unpaid work on nurses' well-being: The importance of gender. *Sociology of Health and Illness*, 19, 328-347.

Ware Jr., J. (1986). The assessment of health status. In: Aiken, L.H. and Mechanic, D. (eds.): *Applications of social science to clinical medicine and health policy*. Rutgers University Press, New Brunswick, N.J., pp 204-228

Wheeler, H., Riding, R. (1994). Occupational stress in general nurses and midwives. *British Journal of Nursing*, 3, 527-534.

Yoder, LH. (1995). Staff nurses' career development relationships and self-reports of professionalism, job satisfaction, and intent to stay. *Nursing Research*, 44, 290-297.

Zammuner, V.L., Galli, C. (2005). Wellbeing: Causes and consequences of emotion regulation in work settings. *International Review of Psychiatry*, 17, 355-364.

In: Industrial Psychology Research Trends
Editor: Ina M. Pearle, pp. 105-119

ISBN: 978-1-60021-825-5
© 2007 Nova Science Publishers, Inc.

*Chapter 6*

# INTERVENTION MEASURES TO DEAL WITH THE IMPACT OF NIGHT AND SHIFTWORK TO WORKERS' HEALTH AND WELL-BEING

*Lucia Rotenberg[1], Claudia Roberta de Castro Moreno[2] and Frida Marina Fischer[2]*

[1] Laboratory of Environment and Health Education,
Oswaldo Cruz, Institute, FIOCRUZ, Brazil.
[2] Department of Environmental Health, School of Public Health,
University of Sao Paulo, Brazil

## ABSTRACT

Night and shiftwork affect the workers' health and psychosocial well-being, due to the disruption of biological rhythms and difficulties adjusting to sociofamily life. Problems related to those work schedules are unavoidable, since working at odd hours is not compatible with the diurnal pattern of the human body and the organization of society. The financial "basic compensation" adopted worldwide is obviously not enough to compensate workers for the inconveniences related to night and shiftwork, as an extra payment does not help them to deal with health hazards, sleep deprivation or to family disruption associated with working non-diurnal shifts. This is why there is a general agreement among researchers that intervention measures should focus on the effective reduction of the impact of these work schedules. There is no general way to achieve this goal. Actually, the selection of measures depends on the specific situation, with emphasis on the reduction of human and social costs by means of measures towards each type of hazard. Thus, intervention measures are not definitive solutions to problems, but instead can be viewed as recommendations and strategies implemented by employees and employers to reduce difficulties related to workers' health and well-being. Such recommendations deal with aspects related to work organization, so as to reduce the demands for shiftwork (mainly night work and irregular working times), or to implement work schemes that imply less problems to workers. Intervention measures also refer to changes in the work environment as, for instance, providing round-the-clock canteens with adequate meals for night workers. Measures aiming at the adjustment of biological rhythms to the work schedule are based on chronobiological principles, such as those related to melatonin ingestion or exposure to bright light. Whatever the action to be adopted, the educational perspective and the participative approach seem to be relevant in dealing with challenges related to night and shiftwork, as judged by successful interventions in several industries and service sectors.

## INTRODUCTION

The 24-hour society is a reality in several urban areas worldwide, due to demands of provision of goods and services throughout the day and night. As a consequence, an increasing number of workers are required to work outside the regular 0800-1700 h working day and this figure is likely to increase (Rajaratnam and Arendt, 2001). The large number of people involved in permanent night and rotating shift work has become an unavoidable attribute of our society nowadays (Haus and Smolensky, 2006).

Night and shift workers suffer from the misalignment between biological rhythms and their work schedule, thus resulting in several consequences to health and well being, such as sleepiness, impaired performance, sleep difficulties, gastrointestinal and cardiovascular disturbances (Knutsson, 2003; Costa, 2003). Recent epidemiological studies showed an association between working shifts and the incidence of breast cancer (Schernhammer et al., 2006; Megdal et al., 2005). These health outcomes add to workers' difficulties adjusting to sociofamily life, derived from the incompatibility between the work schedule and the family/social engagements. In addition, night and shift workers are at a high risk of injuries and accidents in industry and transport (Philip, 2005; Philip and Akerstedt, 2006). Thus, Moreno and Louzada (2004) refer to night and shiftworkers as those who are "swimming against the tide" (Moreno and Louzada, 2004, p. 1740). The psychophysiological consequences of those work schedules are explained by Chronobiology, the branch of science especially dealing with biological rhythms. The harmful effects of night and shiftwork are inevitable, as their corresponding work schedules contradict the 24-h organization of human body and society (Monk, 2000). Within this context, intervention measures are not definitive solutions to problems, but instead can be viewed as recommendations aiming at minimizing difficulties related to workers' physical and mental health and well-being, as described in the next sections.

## INTERVENTION AND STRATEGIES TO ALLEVIATE PROBLEMS RELATED TO NIGHT AND SHIFT WORK

### The Countervalue Model: What an Intervention Should Be

An essential issue in dealing with intervention measures related to night and shiftwork is that the extra payment, adopted worldwide as a basic "compensation" for the inconveniences of night work, is not sufficient to compensate for the stress that workers are exposed to: paying extra money to an individual does not necessarily help him/her to sleep better, neither does it help them deal better with inevitable family problems. The distinction between counterweight and countervalue interventions was introduced in the 1970's by Dutch researchers (Thierry et al., 1975), according to whom, the bonus amount corresponds to a counterweight measure, in the sense that it does not change the drawbacks of working atypical hours. On the other hand, in offering countervalue, interventions are chosen that try to deal with, as best as possible, the relevant complaints. In this regard, interventions that contribute to minimize the impact of work schedules, such as with, regular medical assistance should be proposed to workers as a means to reduce the effects of shiftwork upon health (Wedderburn, 1991a). The merit of the countervalue measure lies on its flexibility, as selection of procedures depends on the concrete situation. Emphasis should be given to a reduction in human and social costs through measures that address each of such costs.

## Changes in Work Schedules

Implementing new shift schedules is a complex task which involves conflicting interests between the social groups participating in the process (Kogi and Di Martino, 1995). In this sense, they should constitute a solution involving a reasonable commitment on the part of employees and employers. This is the reason why it demands negotiations between the parties and, ideally, a joint planning (Knauth, 1996). The need that employees participate in the planning of new temporal arrangements is emphasized by Knauth (2001) when he discusses positive and negative experiences involving the development and implementation of shift schedules.

The analysis of participative processes in different countries reveals that the most successful practices are those that rely on an effective support, which is translated into (a) collecting data on the company's operating demands and the employees needs and preferences through questionnaires, interviews, group discussions; (b) establishment of work groups that would include workers representatives qualified to identify local demands; and (c) training external partners capable of facilitating the task and the negotiations necessary to reach a consensus; this is a critical point, as the agreements that would have to be settled involve conflicting interests. Upon delivering the results of the change from slow alternating shifts (8-hour shifts) to rapid alternating shifts (8 or 12 hours), Smith et al. (1998a) highlight the support to the change as a critical factor for the change to produce a positive impact on workers welfare.

Besides emphasizing the relevance of workers participation, Knauth (2001) mentions other points that have been considered paramount to the success of the changes intended, such as:

- aspects related to information and communication: if it is confirmed that the new scheme provides greater autonomy, workers and managers would have to be trained to deal with the new situation;
- commitment to such changes of general managers, supervisors, the community of workers and, if necessary, of external consultants;
- a clear definition of the project objectives;
- synergy between company objectives, workers wishes and the ergonomic demands that regulate the development of shift schedules;
- an adequate organizational structure, which would include a planning phase extending through at least six months and a pilot phase covering one year.

Changes in shift schedules should be limited, and should be implemented gradually; in addition, they should be reversible. Their objectives, as well as their potential impacts, should be clearly expressed. They should be introduced in situations where there is no work overload and under a favorable social atmosphere. Ideally, they should not be motivated exclusively by employee's interests (Wedderburn, 1994).

There is not an "optimal" shift schedule. Each schedule has its advantages and drawbacks in relation to physical, psychological or social welfare (Knauth, 1993). International entities dedicated to the improvement of workers qualify of life – such as the *"European Foundation for the Improvement of Living and Working Conditions"* – have ergonomic recommendations that aim at humanizing shift schedules (Wedderburn, 1991b).

One of these recommendations says that night workload shouldn't be too demanding. Increasing the number of days off, early retirement or transfer to day shifts constitute other ways of reaching this intent, as discussed below. Some of these measures provide the worker the opportunity to compensate for problems related to sleep and to perform household tasks when he/she does not have to work extra hours or does not have a second job (Wedderburn, 1991b).

Reducing the number of fixed night shifts is a critical recommendation and, in case this is not feasible, it is suggested that the number of consecutive night shifts be reduced to a minimum – from two to four nights at most (Knauth, 1996). Following each sequence of night shifts the employee should have at least two days off, since the first 24 hours subsequent to the last night shift corresponds to a moment of extreme fatigue, as remarked by Akerstedt (1996).

The speed of shift rotation is another important factor. Although there isn't a consensus among authors, they somehow agree as to the preference for rapid rotating shifts (Akerstedt, 1996), as they cause limited changes in circadian rhythms (Costa et al., 1994) and a lower sleep deficit (Williamson and Sanderson, 1986, Tepas and Mahan, 1989), in addition to benefiting the worker's social life (Knauth e Schönfelder, 1990).

The time when morning shifts start should also be taken into consideration in view of the reduction in sleep on the night preceding the morning shift, particularly when it starts too early. This recommendation is based on the confirmation that in general people have difficulties in falling asleep early even when they have to wake up early the following morning. This "reluctance" is due not only to social pressures to remain awaken (a), but also to the characteristics of their biological clock, which prevents them from going to be much earlier than they usually do (Folkard and Barton, 1993).

The day off between work shifts should not be below 11 hours, as intervals shorter than that are associated with a greater sleep deficit. Allocation of days off is extremely important in view of the social value attributed to time, according to which days off that fall on weekends have greater value. Thus, working on weekends should be avoided or, in cases of continuous schedules, blocks of days off should be allocated to weekends whenever possible.

Landrigan et al. (2004) described an interesting intervention related to the association between night work and long work hours (24-hour work shifts or more) in interns at an intensive care unit. The authors showed that reducing the number of hours worked per week significantly contributed to the reduction in serious medical errors, thus reducing risks to the patients.

The compressed workweek is a current trend in some production segments, such as chemical and petrochemical industry, oil off-shore plataforms, steel plants, medical services, cargo transportation, amongst others. In this case, the person works for a period above 8 hours/day, and this results in a week covering less than 5 work days (Tepas, 1985). This theme has been subject to special attention in discussions about work in industries, in view of the current trend towards the adoption of 12- or 10-hour shifts in substitution for 8-hour shifts (Axelsson et al., 1998; Lowden et al., 1998. This – which, in essence, contradicts the struggle undertaken by workers for a 8-hour shifts (Langenfelt, 1974, according to Tepas, 1985) – has motivated debates among specialists with regard to the advantages and drawbacks arising from such long daily shifts (Caruso et al, 2004, Caruso, 2006).

Several authors refer to the popularity these schedules have enjoyed among workers, in view of the larger number of days off and the lower number of days the employee has to go to work, which leads to a reduction in expenses, as well in the time spent in transportation (Wedderburn, 1997; Akerstedt and Kecklund, 2005). Nevertheless, in several situations the negative effects related to fatigue added to the risk involving safety are important factors to be considered (Smith at al., 1998b). It is worth pointing out the complexity involving these studies, in view of the need to take also into consideration sleep patterns, physical health and psychosocial wellbeing, worker's performance, absenteeism rates, aspects related to implementation of the change process, attitudes adopted by professionals, and their preferences, besides factors related to a second job. In Knauth's opinion (1996), 12-hour shifts should be implemented only if the nature of work and the workload are adequate to activities of extended duration, if the schedule is planned to minimize extreme fatigue, if there are arrangements to cover absences, and if there is no need to work extra hours (Caruso, 2004).

An increasing trend in terms of work organization is the adoption of flexible schedules, which would include daily shifts with varying duration, customized schedules, combination of part-time and full time schedules, task-sharing, and temporary transfer to day shifts. This is an important theme included in practical approaches related to the development of work schedules which favor health and, on a broader scope, workers tolerance (Kogi, 1995; Kogi e Di Martino, 1995). In spite of the current popularity of flexible working hours, some of those arrangements are known to be related to impairing effects to health and well being (Giebel et al., 2004; Janssen and Nachreiner, 2004). This apparent contradiction may result from the lack of a suitable and generally accepted definition of flexible work hours, the most obvious distinction is where the influence over the working hours lies, between the "company-based flexibility" and the "individual-oriented flexibility", as observed by Costa et al. (2004). These authors conclude that there is a strong need for a systematic research for evaluating what and where are the positive effects of flexible working hous, particularly, as concerns workers' autonomy.

It is impossible to reconcile all recommendations based on ergonomic and chronobiological criteria. Analyzing the pros and cons related to shift schedules is a complex job, in view of the several variables involved. Several instruments have been developed with the purpose of providing a general assessment of work schedules based on their compliance or non-compliance with the above-mentioned recommendations. Within this context, the role played by new softwares is critical both for the evaluation of shift schedules and the development of new work schemes, as described by Schomann et al. (2004) and Gartner et al. (2004).

## Measures Specifically Related to Sleep and Alertness at Work

Since sleep deprivation is a central issue for shiftworkers, recommendations referring to sleeping habits are crucial to favor their sleep or alertness conditions. Naps are considered quite important within this context, acting as a strategy to deal with situations that demand alertness, and they may be taken before work or during the work shift (Rosekind at al., 1995; Arora et al., 2006; Smith-Coggins et al., 2006). Several field studies describe the advantages of the so-called planned naps for mitigating drowsiness and improve performance and alertness in truckers (Adams-Guppy and Guppy, 2003), interns (Arora et al., 2006), physicians and.nurses (Smith-Coggins et al., 2006).

Although permission to sleep during the night shift may seem utopian it may be essential to reduce sleepiness and night fatigue. The prevalence of naps between shifts is high among several professional categories; a survey on sleep patterns carried out in Japan with night workers showed that 40% of this population takes naps during their shifts, either in function of collective agreements or informally, with the management implied permission (Kogi, 2000). If it is not possible to implement such measure in every situation, it should then be implemented whenever the work conditions allows it. A short sleep during the night shift may have positive effects upon performance, on the adjustment of biological rhythms and on tolerance to shiftwork, showing that "one hour of sleep during the work shift is more important than several hours fighting sleep" (Knauth at al., 1989). Some other specialists consider that this theme deserves further studies (Tepas, 2000).

Upon analyzing naps as a means to prevent fatigue and sleepiness in operational environments, Rosekind at al., (1995) refer to their efficacy in improving performance and alertness, based on results from research carried out. They point out, however, the negative aspects of naps, that is, the harmful effect on subsequent sleep and the so called "sleep inertia" (sleepiness and worse performance immediately after waking up), which should be carefully considered upon planning such actions.

As for the increase in alertness, no conclusive data about the effectiveness of medications utilized in occupational environments are available, as per conclusion reached by Akerstedt and Ficca (1997) based on a revision of the theme. Ingestion of caffeine may counterbalance sleepiness (Walsh, 1995), but information about the best strategy for its consumption is scarce (Alerstedt, 1995). A recent investigation by Jay et al. (2006) showed that a caffeinated energy drink is effective in counteracting sleepiness in a simulated single night-shift, but the authors recognize the need for new investigations over successive working nights.

In the specific case of drivers, the most effective practice to counterbalance sleepiness while driving is, no doubt, to stop driving as soon as possible. Some actions that could be taken while driving – such as opening the window to get fresh air or increasing the radio volume – may be useful meanwhile the professional tries to find a place to park and rest for a while (Horne e Reyner, 1995).

## Measures Related to Sleep at Home

Although diurnal sleep is negatively impacted by physiological and environmental factors, up to a certain extent it is possible to adjust the so called "sleep hygiene" in the case of shiftworkers. Sleep hygiene corresponds to behavioral patterns utilized with the purpose of maintaining favorable sleeping habits, which are valid to any individual. These patterns encompass sleep environmental aspects, such as absence of noise and light, a pleasant temperature, quality of bed and mattress, as well as behavioral issues, such as organization of sleep schedules that match, as much as possible, the normal sleeping schedule. Other patterns include restrictions to ingestion of alcoholic drinks and coffee before going to bed (Rosa et al., 1990; Akerstedt, 1996; Stone and Turner, 1997).

Agreements set between employees and employers may lead to the adoption of effective measures that favor the employee's sleep. As an example we could mention the innovations implemented by a chemical industry in Germany, which insured the construction of sound-proof rooms and priority for shiftworkers to acquire apartment houses in quiet residential areas (Wedderburn, 1991a).

The occasional use of hypnotic drugs can minimize difficulties related to shiftworkers sleep and those who take transmeridian flights. Selection of the medication should take into consideration the duration of the drug effect and its possible side effects, as pointed out by Stone and Turner (1997). However, it should noted that this is an individual solution, since the use of drugs would hardly be accepted as a means to eliminate factors that are inherent to the normal work environment (Akerstedt, 1995). It must be emphasized that care should be taken regarding non prescribed medications, unless such medications do not involve any type of residual effect (Stone and Turner, 1997). No matter the medication selected, its utilization by shiftworkers should be established in function of its effect not only upon sleep, but also upon alertness at work (Costa at al., 1994).

## Measures Related to the Adjustment of Biological Rhythms

In recent years, two types of interventions have been investigated with the purpose of favoring the physiological adjustment to night work: oral administration of melatonin and use of high intensity light sources, the so called "bright light".

Melatonin is a natural hormone secreted by the pineal gland. This substance acts upon our biological clock and, when supplied at certain times, can improve shiftworkers sleep, having also other beneficial effects. The correct use of this substance may contribute to minimize some of the problems faced by shiftworkers, particularly improving the sleep quality and alertness conditions, thus facilitating their adaptation to the work schedule (Arendt et al, 1995; Arendt and Deacon, 1997). However, these authors point out that the effects of melatonin upon performance and sleep architecture (quality) deserve further studies; they also recommend that research is carried out aiming at dosage and formulation optimization.

Melatonin can also be utilized to minimize jet-lag symptoms, particularly in relation to sleep (Arendt et al, 1995). In spite of this, some authors do not recommend the use of this substance by the crew, only by passengers, as in their view, administration of melatonin at bed time, on the place of destination, can improve sleep quality and reduce the time the circadian rhythms need to adjust (Sanders et al, 1999). These authors consider that the use of melatonin can be harmful to the crew, as its members do not have enough time to adapt to the new environment, thus making still more difficult the adjustment of circadian rhythms.

The use of bright light as a means to favor adaptation to work schedule is based on the role of the light-dark cycle as a synchronizer of the circadian system. The effects of light on the circadian system are determined by several factors: intensity, wavelength, and duration of the light exposure (Smith et al, 2004; Thapan et al, 2001; Zeitzer et al, 2000). Also, the prior light exposure history can have an effect upon the circadian system (Rimmer et al, 2000). This fact is particularly relevant to understand the association of these effects and aging. Recent findings suggest an age-related reduction in the phase-delaying response to moderate light levels of exposure (Duffy at al, 2006).

On the other hand, the consensus among the researchers that the effect of light exposure on the circadian system is time-dependent is not a new finding. On the 70's Daan and Pittendrigh (1976), and also Wever (1979) had already shown the influence of light exposure on the circadian system. The confirmation that the circadian rhythms could be adjusted by manipulation of light sources has led to the development of a technology that applies bright light in work environments, which results in the improvement of the workers alertness status during night work, as well as their sleep quality and welfare (Ehrenstein, 2000; Eastman and Martin, 1999). This technology was first applied in NASA operations; its benefits have been recognized by workers themselves, and are currently used in all missions (Czeisler and Dijk, 1995).

However, specialists in the area recognize the light levels required to maintain human circadian phase in the absence of other strong time cues are still unknown (Middleton et al, 2002). It is necessary to carry out large-scale field studies, so as to evaluate the efficacy in several different shifts, and to adapt the use of this technology to the worker's social demands, operational needs and biological characteristics involving the regulation of the circadian system (Czeisler and Dijk, 1995).

In the case of jet lag symptoms, doubts about the actual benefits of intense light still remain, as remarked by Samel and Wegmann (1997) on a review about the theme. In another review, Burgess at al (2002) pointed out the main findings which could promote the circadian adaptation to night work, among them, 1) the use of exogenous melatonin when phases advances of the circadian system are needed; 2) appropriately timed patterns of medium intensity and/or intermittent light during night work; 3) dark sunglasses when travelling home from the night shift.

## Medical Surveillance

Costa (1998) recommends that tolerance to shift schedules should be evaluated by medical doctors specialized in occupational health before the worker joins the shift, from time to time along the time he/she is engaged in shiftwork, and whenever a health problem arises or is aggravated as a result of the work schedule. Such evaluations should be coupled with a careful ergonomic work analysis, so as to check if a given shift scheme is organized in accordance with ergonomic criteria. According to Costa (1998), this procedure might contribute to minimize health problems, allowing adaptation to work, even when the presence of a given illness counter indicates shiftwork.

Periodical medical evaluations are critical, considering that this is a population subject to risk. These evaluations should be oriented to early detection of symptoms involving intolerance, such as digestive, sleep, and reproductive disturbances, drug consumption, work accidents and incidents, socio-family problems. Some issues that talk about tolerance to shiftwork should be taken into consideration, such as specific working conditions, individual characteristics and social factors impacting tolerance to night work and shiftwork (Costa, 1999). Nevertheless, it should be emphasized that health monitoring should not be limited to the control of symptoms related to chronic problems; monitoring should include counseling and recommendations oriented to the performance of shift work, pursuant to Wedderburn's (1991b) recommendations. Attention should also be given to elderly workers, who may require closer assistance. Aging workers may experience more difficulties to change day to night work, as well as have an aggravation on sleep disturbances.

## Other Measures Related the Work Environment and/or to the Worker's Behavior

Providing round-the-clock canteens that cater adequatetly for the meal needs of night workers is a simple measure that can be successfully implemented by employers. This can be done in connection with a nutrition education program, so as to avoid the use of vending machines that contribute to workers' poor diet (Stewart and Wahlqvist, 1985).

The physical conditioning has been proposed by Harma et al. (1998a, b) as a means to improve tolerance to night work and shiftwork by gradually increasing adjustment to the work schedule. Upon following up the results of physical training programs carried out with nurses who worked in alternating shifts, the authors observed positive effects of exercises, such as reduction in general fatigue, as well as in skeletal muscle symptoms, and an increase in sleep duration after the evening shift. Nevertheless, other authors, such as Redlin and Mrosovsky (1997), highlight the scarcity of studies in this area, considering premature any specific recommendation on the use of physical exercises to favor the synchronization of biological rhythms.

## TRANSFORMING SCIENTIFIC KNOWLEDGE INTO PRACTICES

An increasing number of workers have benefited from Chronobiology with respect to recommendations on nutrition, sleep hygiene, health and family life (Monk, 2000). This knowledge, jointly with those obtained from Ergonomics, make up a mass of information which couple human physiology and work organizational aspects with the purpose of improving the worker and his/her family quality of life.

The impact of lifestyle education and training for work hours has long been studied,including the implementation of programs that provide orientation to workers and their families (Tepas, 1993; Kerin and Aguirre, 2005). Roughly speaking, educational actions involve the development of informational materials approaching behaviors related to sleep, nutrition, practice of physical exercises and family life (Rankin and Wedderburn, 2000).

The educational materials include articles published in magazines oriented to professional groups (such as policemen and nurses) and manuals ("guidelines") written by researchers in the area, such as *Guidelines for Shiftworkers* published by the European Foundation for Improvement of Work and Living Conditions (Wedderburn, 1991b), in addition to booklets developed by companies working specifically with this theme, such as "*Circadian Technologies, Inc Company*. Yet, these techniques haven't been well evaluated in terms of their efficacy for the population they are intended (Rankin and Wedderburn, 2000). According to Wedderburn (1993), specialists should be more careful when giving "advice" which, in practice, hasn't demonstrated to be better than that provided by more experienced workers. Far from denying the need for regulations that are based on scientific knowledge, the author calls attention to the challenge that lies in demonstrating that such recommendations are better than those empirically dictated by life experience.

The analysis of intervention educational programs shows to which extent their success depends on workers active participation, as already demonstrated by some experiences. Turner (1995), for instance, described a pilot project based on an initiative taken by a group of nurses which, in turn, was based on their sound experience in shiftwork and on results of research carried out in the area. The project dealt with difficulties related to sleep and nutrition, and was based on a detailed quantitative and qualitative survey on sleep and nutrition habits carried out by the professionals involved. Using this material and relying on the help of nutritionists, a workshop was held for discussion of the most problematic issues, including sleep aspects, diet composition (the nurses learned to analyze the content of their diet) and individual strategies to deal with problems deriving from the work schedule. The project lasted for five months, and resulted in a significant improvement in sleep, health and psychological welfare of all nurses.

Interviews with groups of nurses to collect their opinions about educational interventions showed their preference for programs geared to groups, rather than individual counseling (Novak and Auvil-Novak, 1996).

Another interesting experience was that of a Japanese company which adopted a counterclockwise scheme with irregular shifts. The intervention program was motivated by the high prevalence of complaints from workers concerning fatigue, back pain, short sleep duration and "irregular" days off. With the participation of workers and the cooperation from their union, researchers and members from the administration, a program was developed with the purpose of analyzing, planning and implementing improvements in the shift rotation scheme. Such program included several methods for data collection, which were afterwards jointly analyzed; it has generated alternative shift schemes incorporating more regular rotations. The experience has demonstrated the importance of adopting gradual intervention strategies that include frequent discussions and a participative process that approaches the large number of issues related to the workers life and health (Sakai at al., 1993).

As it can be seen, the educational approach should be oriented to both employers and employees, no matter the measure to be taken. Under the employer's viewpoint, it should focus on the economic impact resulting from high workers turnover and absenteeism, showing the advantages of adopting a more humane focus when dealing with shiftwork. As for employees, the educational approach may help them understand that not necessarily they are weak, sick, or have an unsatisfactory marriage (Monk and Folkard, 1992).

## CONCLUSION

Nowadays, occupational health interventions show a clear trend toward joint approaches to improve both safety and health management. This is a consequence of the growing evidence that safer and healthier shiftwork conditions require not only changes in working time arrangements, but also the adequate management of other workplace risks (Kogi, 2004). The current regulation of issues related to health and safety in the work environment presumes the existence of an environmental and organizational structure that ensures better health conditions and defines the obligations and rights of the parties involved. The concern with issues related to health upon planning shifts reflects the importance of developing participative processes and establishing joint committees as a means to protect the worker's rights with regard to working conditions and factors related to health and safety in the work environment (Jeppesen and Boggild, 1998).

The relevance of employees participation in the analysis of work shifts can be inferred through the field study carried out by Sluiter et al. (2005) in an intensive care unit. The authors described a multidisciplinary structured work shift evaluation that was successfully tested among physicians and nurses, contributing to enhance team communication.

The large-scale change in working hours ongoing in our society (Costa et al., 2004) leads to an increasing number of people involved in some kind of work shift, thus demanding the implementation of policies to reduce the impact of night and rotating shifts to workers' health and psychosocial well-being. Those policies should consider the general aging of the working population (Harma et al., 2006) as well as their engagement in precarious employment with potential impact on workers' health (Bohle et al., 2004).

It is up to the society as a whole, which benefits from around-the-clock services, to mobilize efforts in the field of research and the legislation geared to humanizing night work and shiftwork. Minimizing problems associated with shift schemes means contributing to transform the work not into something that brings suffering, but which represents a source of pleasure and improvement of life quality.

# REFERENCES

Adams-Guppy J, Guppy A. Truck driver fatigue risk assessment and management: a multinational survey. *Ergonomics* 2003; 46: 763-779.

Akerstedt T, Kecklund G. The future of work hours - the European view. *Ind Health* 2005;43: 80-4.

Akerstedt, T. 1995. Work hours, sleepines and accidents. Introduction and summary. *J. Sleep Res.*, 4, suppl. 2: 1-3.

Akerstedt, T. e Ficca, G., 1997. Alertness-enhancing drugs as a countermeasure to fatigue in irregular work hours. *Chronobiol. Int.*, 14: 145-158.

Akerstedt, T., 1996. *Wide awake at odd hours. Shift work, time zones and burning the midnight oil.* Swedish Council for Work Life Research, Estocolmo.

Arora V, Dunphy C, Chang VY, Ahmad F, Hum´phrey HJ, Meltzer D. The effects of on-duty napping on intern sleep time and fatigue. *Ann. Intern. Med.* 2006; 144: 792-798.

Axelsson, J., Kecklund, G., Akerstedt, T., Lowden, A., 1998. Effects of alternating 8 and 12-hour shifts on sleep, sleepiness, physical effort and performance. *Scand. J. Work Environ Health*, 24, suppl. 3: 62-68.

Bohle P, Quinlan M, Kennedy D, Williamson A. Working hours, work-life conflict and health in precarious and "permanent" employment. *Rev. Saude Publica.* 2004;38 Suppl 19-25.

Burgess HJ, Sharkey KM, Eastman CI. Bright light, dark and melatonin can promote circadian adaptation in night shift workers. *Sleep Medicine Review* 2002; 6(5): 407-420.

Caruso C C. Possible broad impacts of long work hours. *Ind. Health* 2006; 44: 531-631.

Caruso CC. Hitchcock EM, Dick RB, Russo JM Schmit JM. *Overtime and extended work shifts: recent findings on illnesses, injuries, and health behaviors.* (NIOSH, Publication No. 2004-143) Department of Health and Human Services, Public Health Service, Centers for Disease Control and Prevention, National Institute for Occupational Safety and Health,Cincinnati, Ohio.

Costa G, Akerstedt T, Nachreiner F, Baltieri F, Carvalhais J, Folkard S, Dresen MF, Gadbois C, Gartner J, Grzech-Sukalo H, Harma M, Kandolin I, Sartori S, Silverio J. Flexible working hours, and well-being in Europe: some considerations from a SALTSA Project. *Chronobiol. Int.* 2004; 21: 831-844.

Costa G. Shift work and occupational medicine: an overview. *Occup Med* 2003; 53: 83-88.

Costa G. Guidelines for the medical surveillance of shift workers. *Scand. J. Work Environ. Health.* 1998; 24, suppl. 3: 151-155.

Costa G.Shift work and health. *Med. Lav.* 1999; 90: 739-751.

Costa G. Ghirlanda G, Tarondi G, Minors D, Waterhouse J. Evatuation of a rapidly rotating shift system for tolerance of nurses to nightwork. *Int. Arch. Occup. Environ. Health.* 1994; 65: 305-311.

Daan S, Pittendrigh CS. A functional analysis of circadian pacemaker in nocturnal rodent. II. The variability of phase response curves. *J. Comp. Physiol. A* 1976; 106:253-66.

Duffy JF, Zeitzer JM, Czeisler CA. Decreased sensitivity to phase-delaying effects of moderate intensity light in older subjects. *Neurobiol. Aging.* 2007; 28(5):799-807.

Eastman CI, Martin SK. How to use light and dark to produce circadian adaptation to night shift work. *Ann. Med.* 1999; 31:87-98.

Folkard S, Barton J. Does the "forbidden zone" for sleep onset influence morning shift sleep duration? *Ergonomics.* 1993; 36: 85-91.

Gartner J, Popkin S, Leitner W, Wahl S, Akerstedt T. Analysing irregular working hours: lessons learned in the development of RAS 1.0 – the representation and analysis software. *Chronob. Int.* 2004; 21: 1025-1035.

Giebel O, Janssen D, Schomann C, Nachreiner F. A new approach for evaluating flexible working hours. *Chronobiol. Int.* 2004;21:1015-1024.

Harma M, Tarja H, Irja K, Mikael S, Jussi V, Anne B, Pertti M. A controlled intervention study on the effects of a very rapidly forward rotating shift system on sleep-wakefulness and well-being among young and elderly shift workers. *Int. J. Psychophysiol.* 2006;59:70-79.

Härmä, M., Ilmarinen, J. e Knauth, P., 1988a. Physical fitness and other individual factors relating to the shiftwork tolerance of women. *Chronobiol. Int.,* 5: 417-424.

Härmä, M., Ilmarinen,J., Knauth, P., Rutenfranz, J. e Hänninen, O., 1988b. Physical training intervention in female shift workers: I. The effects of intervention on fitness, fatigue, sleep and psychosomatic symptoms. *Ergonomics,* 31: 39-50.

Haus E, Smolensky M. Biological clocks and shift work: circadian dysregulation and potential long-term effects. *Cancer Causes Control* 2006;17:489-500.

Horne JA, Reyner, LA. Driver sleepiness. *J. Sleep Res* 1995; 4, suppl. 2: 23-29.

Janssen D, Nachreiner F. Health and psychosocial effects of flexible working hours. *Rev. Saude Publica.* 2004;38 Suppl:11-18.

Jay SM, Petrilli RM, Ferguson SA, Dawson D, Lamond N. The suitability of a caffeinated energy drink for night-shift workers. *Physiol. Behav.* 2006; 87: 925-931.

Jeppesen HJ, Boggild H. Management of health and safety in the organization of working at the local level. *Scand. J. Work Environ. Health* 1998; 24, suppl. 3: 81-88.

Kerin A, Aguirre A. Improving health, safety, and profits in extended hours operations (shiftwork). *Ind. Health* 2005;43:201-208.

Knauth, P, Rutenfranz, J, Fischer, FM. *Trabalho em turnos e noturno.* Hucitec, 1989. São Paulo, Brazil.

Knauth P, Schönfelder E. Effects of a new shift system on the social life of shiftworkers. In: *Studies in Industrial Organizational Psychology – Shiftwork health, sleep and performance.* G. Costa G, Cesana K Kogi e A. Wedderburn (eds.), Frankfurt, Peter Lang 1990. 10: 537-545.

Knauth P. The design of shift systems. *Ergonomics.* 1993; 36: 15-28.

Knauth P. Design of shiftwork systems. *In:* W.P. Colquhoun, G. Costa, S. Folkard, P. Knauth (eds.) *Shiftwork: problems and solutions.* Peter Lang Verlag Frankfurt Main, 1996; p. 155-174.

Knauth P. The process of introducing new shift systems. *Shiftwork Int. Newsletter* 2001; 18: 2.

Knutsson A. Health disorders of shift workers. *Occup. Med.* 2003; 53: 103-108.

Kogi K, Di Martino VG. Trends in the participatory process of changing shiftwork arrangements. *Work and Stress.*1995; 9: 298-304.

Kogi K. Increasing flexibility in shiftwork arrangements. *Work and Stress* 1995; 9: 211-218.

Kogi K. Linking better shiftwork arrangements with safety and health management systems. *Rev. Saude Publica.* 2004;38 Suppl:72-79.

Kogi K. Should shiftworkers nap? Spread, roles and effects of on-duty napping. *Arbeitswissenschaft in der betrieblichen Praxis.* 2000; 17: 31-36.

Landrigan CP, Rothschild JM, Cronin JW, Kaushal R, Burdick E, Katz JT, Lilli CM, Stone PH, Lockley SW, Bates DW, Czeisler CA. Effect of reducing interns' work hours on serious medical errors in intensive care units. *N. Engl. J. Med.* 2004; 351: 1838-1848.

Langenfeld G. *The historic origin of the eight hours day.* Westport, Conn., Greenwood Press. 1974.

Lowden A, Kecklund G, Axelsson J, Akerstedt T. Change from na 8-hour shift to a 12-hour shift: attitudes, sleep, sleepiness and performance. *Scand. J. Work Environ. Health.* 1998; 24, suppl. 3: 69-75.

Megdal SP, Kroenke CH, Laden F, Pukkala E, Schernhammer ES. Night work and breast cancer risk: a systematic review and meta-analysis. *Eur. J. Cancer.* 2005; 41: 2023-2032.

Middleton B, Stone BM, Arendt J. Human circadian phase in 12:12 h, 200: < 8 lux and 1000: < 8 lux light-dark cycles, without scheduled sleep or activity. *Neurosci. Lett.* 2002; 329: 41-44.

Monk T., Folkard S. *Making shift work tolerable.* Taylor and Francis, Londres, 1992.

Monk T. What can the chronobiologist do to help the shift worker? *J. Biol. Rhythms.* 2000; 15: 86-94.

Moreno CR, Louzada FM. What happens to the body when one works at night? *Cad. Saude Publica.* 2004;20:1739-1745

Novak RD, Auvil-Novak SE. Focus group evaluation of night nurse shiftwork difficulties and coping strategies. *Chronobiol. Int.* 1996; 13: 457-463.

Philip P, Akerstedt T. Transport and industrial safety, how are they affected by sleepiness and sleep restriction? *Sleep Med. Rev.* 2006;10: 347-356

Philip P. Sleepiness of occupational drivers. *Ind. Health.* 2005;43: 30-33.

Rajaratnam SM, Arendt J. Health in a 24-h society. *Lancet.* 2001;358:999-1005.

Rankin AD, Wedderburn A. Evaluation of a shiftworkers guide. *Arbeitswissenschaft in der betrieblichen Praxis,* 17: 405-410, 2000.

Redlin U, Mrosovsky N. Exercice and human circadian rhythms: what we know and what we need to know. *Chronobiol. Int.* 1997; 14: 221-229.

Rimmer DW, Boivin DB, Shanahan TL, Kronauer RE, Duffy JF, Czeisler CA. Dynamic resetting of the human pacemaker by intermittent bright light. *Am. J. Physiol.* 2000; 279:R1574-9.

Rosa RR, Bonnet MH, Bootzin RR, Eastman CI, Monk T, Penn PT, Tepas DI, Walsh JK. Intervention factors for promoting adjustment to nightwork and shiftwork. *Occup. Med.,* 1990; 5: 391-415.

Rosekind, M.R., Smith, R.J., Miller, D.L., Co, E.L. e Gregory, K.B., 1995. Alertness management: strategic naps in operational settings. *J. Sleep Res.,* 4, suppl. 2: 62-66.

Sakai K, Watanabe A, Kogi K. Educational and intervention strategies for improving a shift system: an experience in a disabled persons facility. *Ergonomics.* 1993; 36: 219-225.

Schernhammer ES, Kroenke CH, Laden F, Hankinson SE. Night work and risk of breast cancer. *Epidemiology.* 2006;17:108-111.

Schomann C, Stapel W, Nickel P, Eden J, Nachreiner F. BASS 4: a software system for ergonomic schedule constitute a preventive strategy? *Journal of Public Health,* 36 (Supp.), 2004; 56-64.

Sluiter JK, Bos AP, Tol D, Calff M, Krijnen M, Frings-Dresen MH. Is staff well-being and communication enhanced by multidisciplinary work shift evaluations? *Intensive Care Med.* 2005;31: 1409-1414.

Smith KA, Schoen MW, Czeisler CA. Adaptation of human pineal melatonin suppression by recent photic history. *J. Clin. Endocrinol. Metab.* 2004; 89:3610-4.

Smith PA, Wright BM, Mackey RW, Milsop HW, Yates SC. Change from slowly rotating 8-hour shifts to rapidly rotating 8-hour and 12-hour shifts using participative shift roster design. *Scand. J. Work Environ. Health.* 1998a; 24, suppl. 3: 55-61.

Smith L, Folkard S, Turcker P, MacDonald I. Work shift duration: a review comparing eight hour and 12 hour shift systems. *Occup. Environ. Med.* 1998b; 55: 217-229.

Smith-Coggins R, Howard SK, Mac DT, Wang C, Kwan S, Rosekind MR, Sowb Y, Balise Stewart, A.J. e Wahlqvist, M.L., 1985. Effect of shiftwork on canteen food purchase. *J. Occup. Med.,* 27: 552-554.

Stone, B.M. e Turner, C., 1997. Promoting sleep in shiftworkers and intercontinental travelers. *Chronobiol. Int.,* 14: 133-143.

Tepas D. Educational programmes for shiftworkers, their families, and prospective shiftworkers. *Ergonomics.* 1993; 36: 199-209.

Tepas, D.I. e Mahan, R.P., 1989. The many meanings of sleep. *Work and Stress,* 3: 93-102.

Tepas DI. Flextime, compressed workweeks and other alternative work schedules. In: *Hours of work – temporal factors in work-scheduling.* S. Folkard e T. Monk (eds.). Chichester, Wiley, p. 147-164. 1985

Tepas DI. Should a general recommendation to nap be made to workers? *Arbeitswissenschaft in der betrieblichen Praxis* 2000; 17: 25-30.

Thapan K, Arendt J, Skene DJ. An action spectrum for melatonin suppression: evidence for a novel non-rod, non-cone photoreceptor system in humans. *J. Physiol.* 2001; 535:261-7.

Thierry HK, Hoolwerf G, Drenth PJD. Attitudes of permanent day and shift workers towards shiftwork – a field study. In: W.P. Coulquhoun, S. Folkard, P. Knauth e J. Rutenfranz (eds.) *Experimental studies of shiftwork.* Verlag, Opladen, 213-231, 1975.

Walsh JK, Muehlbach MJ, Schweitzer PK. Hypnotics and caffeine as countermeasures for shiftwork-related sleepiness and sleep disturbance. *J Sleep Res* 1995; 4, suppl. 2: 80-83.

Wedderburn A. *Compensation for shiftwork.* European Foundation for the Improvement of Living and Working Conditions. Loughlinstown House, Dublin, 1991a.

Wedderburn A. *Guidelines for shiftworkers.* European Foundation for the Improvement of Living and Working Conditions. Loughlinstown House, Dublin, 1991b.

Wedderburn A. *Instruments for designing, implementing and assessing working time arrangements.* European Foundation for the Improvement of Living and Working Conditions. Loughlinstown House, Dublin, 1994.

Wedderburn A *La semaine de travail comprimee.* Foundation Europenne pour l'Amelioration des Conditions de Vie et de Travail. Dublin, 1997.

Wedderburn A. Teaching grandmothers how to sck eggs: Do shiftworkers need rules or guidelines? *Ergonomics* 1993; 36: 239-246.

Wever R. *The circadian system of man.* Berlin, Heidelberg, New York: Springer; 1979.

Williamson AM, Sanderson JW. Changing the speed of shift rotation: a field study. *Ergonomics* 1986: 29: 1085-1096.

Zeitzer JM, Dijk DJ, Kronauer RE, Brown EN, Czeisler CA. Sensitivity of the human circadian pacemaker to nocturnal light: melatonin phase resetting and suppression. *J. Physiol.* 2000; 526: 695-702.

# INDEX

### D

## E

## F

**N**

**O**

**P**

## Q

## R

## S

**Y**